D0392428

NA
9201
W85
1976

134224

N.L. TERTELING LIBRARY
THE COLLEGE OF IDAHO
CALDWELL, IDAHO

HOW THE GREEKS BUILT CITIES

BY

R. E. WYCHERLEY

Second Edition

W · W · NORTON & COMPANY

New York · London

4419 47

NA 9201
W85
1976

W. W. Norton & Company, Inc., 500 Fifth Avenue, New York, N.Y. 10110
W. W. Norton & Company Ltd., 37 Great Russell Street, London WC1B 3NU

Copyright © 1962 by R. E. Wycherley. All rights reserved. Printed in the United
States of America. First published in the Norton Library 1976 by arrangement with St.
Martin's Press.

Books That Live
The Norton imprint on a book means that in the publisher's
estimation it is a book not for a single season but for the years.
W. W. Norton & Company, Inc.

Library of Congress Cataloging in Publication Data

Wycherley, Richard Ernest.
    How the Greeks built cities.

    (The Norton library)
    Reprint of the ed. published by Macmillan, London.
    Bibliography: p.
    Includes index.
    1. Cities and towns—Planning—Greece. 2. Archi-
tecture—Greece. I. Title.
NA9201.W85 1976   711'.4'0938   76-10762

ISBN 0-393-00814-2

1 2 3 4 5 6 7 8 9 0
134224

PREFACE TO SECOND EDITION

THE nineteen-fifties have seen a phenomenal renewal of archaeological investigation in Greek lands. The annual *Archaeological Reports* published by the Hellenic Society and the British School at Athens give a useful conspectus of this work and show its astonishing range and variety. Professor J. M. Cook's report on Greek Archaeology in Western Asia Minor (1960) is especially full of interest for the history of the art which can best be described by the modern Greek word *poleo-domike*.

Much new light has been thrown on the antecedents, origins and prototypes of the Greek city, though this light is often fitful or kaleidoscopic, and for the later periods a mass of new illustrative material has been found. In spite of all this I had no desire to re-write this book completely. Our idea of the classical Hellenic city as a whole and of its principal elements remains essentially the same. When Professor R. Martin's excellent book *L'Urbanisme dans la Grèce Antique* appeared in 1956, I found myself in heartfelt agreement with almost every word of his *Conclusion*.

Changes in the main body of the text have been kept to a minimum ; but many new or improved plans, and a few new photographs, have been substituted for the old ones ; and an extensive series of supplementary notes draws attention to some of the most helpful recent work, on particular sites and in general studies, and briefly indicates its importance.

The work of revision has benefited greatly from a period spent at the Institute for Advanced Study at Princeton, and from two visits to Greece assisted by generous grants from the American Philosophical Society of

Nʸ ʸ̶ᴬᴿʸ
THE COLLEGE OF IDAHO
CALDWELL, IDAHO

Philadelphia. At Athens Professor H. A. Thompson and his colleagues in the agora have been very helpful as always ; Mr. J. Travlos in particular has generously supplied me with material. Mr. Henry Robinson, Director of the American School at Athens, kindly provided me with copies of a series of plans of the agora district of Corinth, by Mr. Travlos ; I am asked to say that these plans, on which fig. 14 is based, were not yet in final form. Mr. I. D. Kondis, of the Department of Antiquities at Athens, sent me much useful material on Rhodes and other sites. Mr. J. Ellis Jones of Bangor drew fig. 2 and fig. 14, and made many suggestions.

For permission to use plans, drawings and photographs I am very grateful to the following : the American School of Classical Studies at Athens, and Mr. J. Travlos (1, 11, 13, 14, 24, 32, 41, 48, XVIa) ; the British School at Athens and the editors of its *Annual* (8) ; the German Archaeological Institute, Athens, and Gebr. Mann Verlag, Berlin (29) ; Mr. I. D. Kondis (26, I) ; Mr. G. P. Stevens and the Royal Ontario Museum, Toronto (VIIb).

When this book was first taking shape I received timely encouragement from Mr. Lewis Mumford ; in introducing this new edition I should like to quote from his latest work *The City in History*. ' The recovery of the essential values that first were incorporated in the ancient cities, above all those of Greece, is a primary condition for the further development of the city in our time.'

UNIVERSITY COLLEGE OF NORTH WALES   R. E. W.
  September 1961

PREFACE TO FIRST EDITION

THE purpose of this brief survey of Hellenic architecture is to define the form of the ancient Greek city and the place of certain elements in it ; and since the place of some of these elements in the whole depends on their own form, I shall add a little about the nature of a number of characteristically Greek building-types, without attempting, however, to cover the whole range. Incidentally, I hope, this treatment will relate architecture more closely to Greek life. All this makes a very ambitious project for a short work, and the result can at best be hardly more than a programme for a series of more thorough and detailed studies. I am conscious of many omissions and much unevenness of treatment, though this is partly due to the difficult conditions of recent years and the inaccessibility of material. There is room for a number of detailed works such as W. A. McDonald's *Meeting-Places of the Greeks*, on particular types of Greek building, as well as for a new study of Greek town-planning to supplement von Gerkan's indispensable work, and I should be glad to furnish further material to anyone working on any of these lines. But I hope that even the present brief treatment will suggest new ways of looking at Greek architecture and raise again the question whether it has not more than a general historical or aesthetic interest nowadays.

The great glory of Greek architecture is the temple. The Greeks dedicated the finest fruits of their artistic genius, and a large proportion of their limited funds and resources, to the gods. The development of the temple

and of the Doric and Ionic orders, which find their
perfect expression in the temple, quite rightly takes first
place in the history of Greek architecture ; the harmonies
and refinements of the orders have an aesthetic value
equal to that of the best sculpture. But although this
beauty can still inspire, it is apt to seem a little remote.
It may help to bring Greek architecture into closer contact
with our own ways of thought if the structure and plan
of the city — the treatment of which is apt to be relegated
to the last chapter — are dealt with first.

Town-planning and town-building are matters of
peculiar interest today ; new towns are being designed
and great old cities are rising in new forms from their
ruins, slowly and with difficulty, as did Athens and
Miletus after the Persian Wars. In these circumstances
the experience of the Greeks, who were great city-builders,
has a renewed interest ; and I think it will be found that
in some things the principles of modern town-planning
are akin to the way of the Greeks. The Greek city, at
its best, was a compact community, capable in itself of
a very high degree of political and cultural life, not overwhelmingly big, organized by and for a large body of
free citizens ; and its outward, architectural form accurately reflected its inner nature. Of course, the conditions
and problems of today are very different, though not
entirely so, and we shall see obvious contrasts at almost
every point. But there is an affinity in general character
which goes deeper than particular analogies, just as ancient
Greek literature has a new significance which cannot be
illustrated by particular quotations from Plato or Thucydides, however 'topical'. It is best to let the facts speak
for themselves ; but perhaps one might say that the

essential link lies in this — the architecture of the *polis* grew out of the needs, ways of life, traditions and ideas of its citizens, and followed these at every point, without pursuing the artificial and the extravagant. Restraint and economy were inevitable.

I shall concentrate on the Hellenic city of the sixth, fifth and fourth centuries, when politically and culturally it was at the highest level of its development ; it will not be necessary to become deeply involved in problems of origins and earlier history, or to cover systematically the succeeding ' Hellenistic ' period ; but I shall inevitably look both backwards and forwards from this view-point from time to time. Hellenic architecture began in a modest way early in the first millennium B.C., but the traditions of the preceding Minoan age were not entirely lost ; and at the other end of the scale, Hippodamian town-planning did not bear its full fruit till Hellenistic times ; some typically Hellenic building-types were architecturally immature in the fifth century — indeed only the temple had reached full maturity — and one has to pursue their history for a further couple of centuries to reach a suitable stopping-point. Peculiarly Hellenistic developments, on the other hand, are outside my present scope.

' Hellenic ', ' Hellenistic ' and such terms are largely conventional, and one's use of them needs definition. The civilization which emerged in Greece in the early centuries of the first millennium B.C. was the result of the super-imposition on an older culture (the ' Minoan ') of a number of new elements which entered in waves from the north. The name Hellenic is most properly applied, I believe, to the final compound, after the last important ingredient had been added and the whole had become comparatively stabilized. At the other end again, after the Macedonian conquest in the latter part of the fourth century, the Greek cities lost something vital, though not without certain gains, and some of the finer qualities of Greek art and architecture evaporated ; and the modified form of Greek culture which is found in the succeeding centuries can be conveniently distinguished as ' Hellenistic ', though the lower limit of the age to which the name is applicable is not clear ; from the first century B.C. onwards, when Roman power had supplanted that of the Hellenistic monarchs in the eastern Mediterranean, one usually speaks of ' Roman ' times in Greece.

Inconsistencies and oddities will be found, I am sure, in my transliteration of Greek names and other Greek words. Unusual strength of mind is required, besides extreme care, if one is to observe strict principles in this matter, and I hardly think I have succeeded.

Full acknowledgment of the source of each plan and photo is made immediately underneath it, the only place where it is sure to be seen. I must thank the Press Board of the University of Wales for a very generous grant towards the cost of assembling materials for the illustrations ; Mr. T. E. Jones and Mr. I. ap Thomas of Bangor for redrawing to my instructions figures 4, 25, 26, 28, 34 and 51 ; and many authors and publishers who have given me permission to use material. I have done my best to make contact with all concerned, but in recent conditions this has sometimes been impossible. In such cases I have still included the material, if its omission would have been a serious loss ; I should like to thank those concerned and shall be very glad to make further amends if opportunity occurs. In taking this course I have been reassured by the invariable generosity and courtesy which I have received, now no less than before the war, from scholars and publishers of all countries. In particular, the man to whom the study of this subject owes more than to any other — A. von Gerkan — says, 'Ich bin der Ansicht, dass publiziertes Material für die Wissenschaft frei sein sollte'. Professor Homer A. Thompson very kindly sent me up-to-date information (September 1947) on the agora of Athens, and new plans and photographs of the new model which had not at the time been published. Professor F. Krischen has allowed me to make free use of his excellent reconstructed drawings of Greek cities. Before the war Dr. H. Schleif readily gave me permission to use for other purposes photos of his carefully constructed models ; this time my letter was returned marked 'Verstorben'. Thanks are also due to the following : Mr. T. J. Dunbabin (Pl. XVI (b)) ; Dr. E. Fiechter (Pl. XIII (a) and fig. 46) ; Dr. A. von Gerkan (numerous plans from *Griechische Städteanlagen* and *Milet*) ; Mr. D. M. Jones (Pls. XII (b) and XVI (a)) ; Professor D. M. Robinson (plans from *Olynthus* ; Professor Robinson has also sent me other useful material on Greek houses) ; Dr. F. Tritsch (fig. 15) ; the Hellenic Society (Pls. III (a), IX, XI, XIV (b), figs. 24, 30) ; the Royal Institute of British Architects (figs. 16, 17 and 23 were originally drawn at the Institute for an article which appeared in the *Journal of the R.I.B.A.*, 17th October 1938 ; the Editor has also very kindly let me have the block from which was printed the plan of Olynthus in the *Journal* of 13th January 1947) ; the Loeb Classical Library and William Heinemann, Ltd. (figs. 1, 24 and 27 ; these plans were originally drawn at the Cambridge Uni-

versity Press for inclusion in vol. v of the Loeb *Pausanias*) ;
the Archaeological Institute of America (figs. 49 and 52) ;
the American School of Classical Studies at Athens (fig.
28 and numerous plans from *Hesperia* ; also Pl. IV) ; the
Metropolitan Museum of Art, New York (Pl. VII (a)) ;
the German Archaeological Institute (Pls. X and XIII (b)) ;
the Clarendon Press, Oxford (figs. 35 and 40) ; E. de
Boccard, Paris (figs. 2, 10 and 48) ; Biederstein Verlag,
München (formerly C. H. Beck) (figs. 1, 32 and 45) ;
Alfred Druckenmüller Verlag (formerly J. B. Metzler)
(fig. 7) ; Verlag Gebr. Mann, Berlin (drawings from
Krischen) ; W. de Gruyter & Co., Berlin (Pls. II (b) and
XII (a), and plans from von Gerkan) ; Deutscher Kunst-
verlag and Staatliche Bildstelle (Pl. III (b)) ; Kunst-
geschichtliches Seminar der Universität Marburg (Lahn)
(Pls. I and VIII (a)).

Finally, I should like to thank the following, if I may
do so without involving them in any kind of responsi-
bility, for suggestions and encouragement given at various
stages of the work : Dr. R. A. Browne, Professor R. A.
Cordingley, Mr. J. A. Davison, Dr. A. von Gerkan, Dr.
A. W. Pickard-Cambridge, Professor D. S. Robertson,
Mr. C. T. Seltman, Dr. F. J. Tritsch, and Professor
T. B. L. Webster ; I am grateful also to my wife for
help with proof-reading and indexing, and to Messrs.
Macmillan, and in particular Mr. H. Cowdell, for the
care they have taken with the production of this work.

On the occasion of the quincentenary of Queens' College, Cambridge, this book is dedicated to members past
and present, and in particular to A. B. Cook.

UNIVERSITY COLLEGE OF NORTH WALES   R. E. W.
December 1947

CONTENTS

Short key bibliographies are given in the first note
of each chapter or subdivision

LIST OF ILLUSTRATIONS

FIGURES IN TEXT

PLATES

ABBREVIATIONS

A.J.A.	= *American Journal of Archaeology.*
Ath. Mit.	= *Mitteilungen des deutschen archäologischen Instituts, Athenische Abteilung.*
B.C.H.	= *Bulletin de Correspondance Hellénique.*
Délos	= T. Homolle, etc., *Exploration archéologique de Délos.*
Fabricius	= Article on Greek Town-planning by E. Fabricius in Pauly-Wissowa, II. Reihe, Halbb. 6, pp. 1982 ff.
von Gerkan	= A. von Gerkan, *Griechische Städteanlagen* (Berlin and Leipzig, 1924).
Jahrbuch	= *Jahrbuch des deutschen archäologischen Instituts.*
J.H.S.	= *Journal of Hellenic Studies.*
Judeich	= W. Judeich, *Topographie von Athen* (2nd edn., Munich, 1931).
Krischen	= F. Krischen, *Die griechische Stadt, Wiederherstellungen* (Berlin, 1938).
McDonald	= W. A. McDonald, *The Political Meeting-places of the Greeks* (Baltimore, 1943).
Milet	= T. Wiegand, etc., *Milet ; Die Ergebnisse der Ausgrabungen und Untersuchungen.*
Ö.J.	= *Jahreshefte des österreichischen archäologischen Instituts in Wien.*
Olynthus	= D. M. Robinson, etc., *Excavations at Olynthus.*
Pauly-Wissowa	= Pauly-Wissowa, *Real-Encyclopädie der classischen Altertumswissenschaft.*
Travlos	= J. Travlos, *Poleodomike Exelixis ton Athenon* (Athens, 1960).
Tritsch, *Elis*	= F. Tritsch, ' Die Agora von Elis und die altgriechische Agora ' (*Ö.J.*, xxvii, pp. 64 ff.).
Weickert, *Typen*	= C. Weickert, *Typen der archaischen Architektur in Griechenland und Kleinasien* (Augsburg, 1929).

INTRODUCTORY

As he neared the end of his *Tour of Greece*, which he made in the second century A.D., Pausanias came to a little place in Phocis called Panopeus. He hesitated to dignify it by the name of 'city' (*polis*) since it possessed 'no government offices or gymnasium, no theatre or agora or water flowing down to a fountain' (x. 4. 1), and consisted merely of a few miserable houses and one or two ancient shrines. Pausanias had visited innumerable cities, large and small, and no one knew better than he what was essential to a Greek city, what gave it its character. In addition he had a method of covering the ground at each important site, omitting nothing 'worth seeing', which makes it easy to see the elements of the city in their proper relation to one another, if one is not distracted by his long historical digressions. We can hardly do better than let him introduce us to our subject. Of course the date at which his descriptions were written is late from our point of view ; but that does not matter. Most of the old cities of European Greece had not changed radically in their general arrangement ; and Pausanias had a strong anti-quarian bias and wrote mainly of what were already ancient monuments in his day.

The visitor who takes Pausanias as his guide approaches by road from his last calling-place, noting interesting monuments by the wayside, including shrines and tombs. As he comes up to the city the dominant feature is the fortification wall, and he may pause to admire its construction. After he has entered one of the main gates the road leads quickly to the heart of the city, the agora. There he finds a large number of buildings, temples and simpler shrines, stoas or colonnades and various other public buildings, interspersed with numerous minor monuments, particularly sculpture. Incidentally, just as Greek sculpture must be placed in its architectural setting to be appreciated, so Greek architecture must be related to sculpture. Pausanias is very helpful in this matter ; he mixes everything up together as he finds it ; one sees the great buildings not standing isolated but embedded in monuments of the lesser arts ; and nowhere more so than in the agora. There the monuments are grouped very loosely round a more or less open area of not very well-defined shape. The effect may be a little confusing or overpowering. In many ancient cities the acropolis rises above, and the visitor will naturally go there next, since some of the most venerable shrines are likely to be found there. The theatre may be built into a suitable part of the lower slopes. Interest will naturally be concentrated on the agora and the acropolis, but things which must not be missed will be found scattered over the rest of the city. The most systematic way of covering the ground is to follow the main streets leading out from the agora to the gates. What one will *not* do with Pausanias is to plunge into the mazes of back streets and dirty alleys where the ordinary houses of ordinary citizens are huddled together. Pausanias fails to satisfy our interest here ; these are not what he calls ' worth seeing '. But fortunately we now know from archaeological evidence much more about Greek houses than we did a few years ago, and we can imagine them filling in the framework which he provides. On the other hand, the abodes of the dead, at least the *famous* dead, appeal to him strongly, and the cemeteries are outside the city gates again, clustered thickly together or strung out along the roads.[1] Other important elements, too, are found in the outskirts or suburbs ; those which need plenty of space, the stadium, for instance, and the gymnasia.

Not all Greek cities were precisely of this form. In particular one must remember that Pausanias confined his attention to old Greece on the European mainland ; in some of the younger colonies new methods were evolved. But everywhere the Greek city consisted architecturally of certain elements essential to its rich and vigorous life. Some of these elements we shall examine in detail ; but first one must briefly consider the question how the city attained the form outlined above and other parallel or modified forms.

GROWTH OF THE GREEK CITY[1]

THE Hellenic city-states grew slowly from modest beginnings in the course of the first half of the first millennium B.C. By the sixth century they had reached a high level of political development and had achieved great things in art and literature. In the latter part of the sixth century and the early years of the fifth the great Persian Empire threatened to engulf them ; but by attaining for a time an unusual degree of unity and by fighting bravely and skilfully they averted the threat ; and in the middle of the fifth century Greece, and especially Athens, rose to still greater heights of achievement. But in the closing decades (431–404 B.C.) nearly the whole Hellenic world was involved in the most disastrous of the wars of Greek against Greek which, with the equally incessant party strife within the cities, constantly sapped the strength of Greece. The fourth century still saw incomparable achievements in art, literature and philosophy ; but the political vigour of the cities was weakening and finally they lost their independence to the rising power of Macedonia (the battle of Chaeronea, 338 B.C., was decisive). However, the ' Hellenistic ' age which followed, when most of the Greek world was dominated by the kingdoms into which the empire of Alexander the Great of Macedon was divided, was by no means a mere age of decadence in the cities, least of all in architecture.

To go back to the beginning — classical Greek civilization crystallized round a nucleus provided by the tradition of an almost equally brilliant predecessor. In the middle of the second millennium B.C., about a thousand years before the heyday of the Greek cities, ' Minoan ' culture was at its height in the Aegean area ; its centre was in Crete. The peoples who ultimately became the Greeks infiltrated into the area in the course of the second millennium. In the earlier phases of the process they adopted the older culture in a modified form, and in time shifted the centre of gravity of the Aegean world from Crete to Mycenae on the European mainland ; but the latest phase of the infiltration (the ' Dorian invasion ') was more destructive, and through its impact and the operation of other causes Minoan-Mycenean culture largely disintegrated.

The relation between the Minoan-Mycenean and Hellenic cultures raises difficult questions which cannot be precisely answered. The cultural thread was not broken, but for several centuries it was frayed and weak, particularly so, I believe, in architecture. It is true that in some ways the Minoan and Mycenean cities foreshadow the Hellenic, though there are almost equally important differences. The Minoan city was concentrated round a centre formed by the palace and a kind of agora, an open place for festal and possibly political gatherings. The Mycenean town was appended to a fortified citadel. F. Tritsch characterizes Minoan and Hellenic cities as both alike centripetal, in contrast with oriental cities, which tend to be centrifugal, with the emphasis on the walls ; and he stresses and perhaps exaggerates the affinity between Minoan and Hellenic.[2] Architecturally the dark middle ages which precede the emergence of the Hellenic cities form an obscure gap. There are hardly any remains of substantial buildings or powerful walls (this is partly due to a reversion to less durable materials). However, many cities grew on sites which had been centres of the earlier civilizations, though there was often a change in relative importance — some of the greater Mycenean centres were of second-rate importance in classical Greece, while lesser sites came to the fore. The massive ' Cyclopean' walls of the earlier fortresses continued to stand and no doubt to be used; and other slighter remains and the persistence of building-types *may* have maintained architectural traditions to some degree. But the Hellenic city was in the main a new thing; its creators had to begin near the beginning, though traditions and survivals provided a nucleus.

At the end of the second millennium and the beginning of the first the level of civilization was comparatively low. Political organization, we may imagine, was rudimentary. There was no great ruler, no Minos or even Agamemnon, exercising wide control, but large numbers of local kings or chiefs. The inhabitants lived in groups of simple village-like communities. Out of a selection of these the Greek cities grew, as the various older and newer elements in Greece settled down to form a more potent political mixture than ever before. The *polis*, the city-state, proved to be the natural expression of this vigorous new spirit; it was larger and offered a richer life than its immediate predecessors, several of which might be absorbed in one city-state, but having reached a certain stage it energetically resisted amalgamation in a larger whole. Geographical conditions, of course, favoured the existence of small and independent states ; Greece is full of great mountain masses, and the more fertile and habitable land consists mainly of small pockets embedded among them or lying between them and the sea, more or less isolated from one another.

While the cities were still taking shape, in the eighth and seventh centuries, strong oriental influences were being brought to bear on Greek culture ; but these influences, though highly stimulating and fruitful, were manifested chiefly in the lesser decorative arts ; the more fundamental art of city building remained purely Hellenic. The general design of the city and the greater architectural forms owed little to oriental or other external influences ; they followed at every step the cultural, religious and political evolution of the Greeks ; new elements were added corresponding to growing and changing needs.

Various factors helped to decide where the cities should grow, and which of the simpler early settlements should be singled out for higher political and architectural development. Natural advantages, of course, played a part, and strategic and economic factors. Sometimes the selection of a place for development as capital, to which lesser towns would now be subordinate, was the deliberate act of a person or group. We must add colonization to the list of processes by which Greek cities came into being ; by this means they spread round Asia Minor and the shores of the Black Sea, and westwards to Italy and Sicily. The colonies were usually complete and autonomous communities from the first. The older were of great antiquity, and developed gradually among the most ancient cities of Greece ; the younger were more deliberately planned and more rapidly developed. Von Gerkan works out a comprehensive classification of Greek cities, according to their origin, which I give in a note ; [3] one must take to heart his warning that the groups are in fact not so neat and tidy, and many cities fall into more than one category.

The historical nucleus of many of the older cities was the *acropolis*, a hill which was defensible without being too high and inaccessible. At an early stage there might be no distinction in meaning between ' polis ' and ' acropolis '. The acropolis was the stronghold which watched over the town and its precious patch of cultivable land, a place of refuge and the seat of the king in the early days when the Greek communities had kings. The rest of the town clustered round its slopes. We can imagine the city as expanding in continually widening circles around the acropolis, or more often on one side of it. The lower city of Athens, Thucydides tells us (ii. 15), shrewdly using the evidence of the monuments, was on the south side originally ; in classical times it had spread all round, forming a ' wheel-shaped ' city (Herodotus vii. 140) with the Acropolis as hub.

The centre of the lower town was the *agora*, for which ' market-place ' is a very inadequate translation, and the rather frigid term ' civic centre ' even worse. ' Market-place ' has obvious limitations, and ' civic centre ' suggests a self-conscious attempt to make one carefully selected bit of the city a token and symbol of its greatness — it has not the intimate association with many familiar things which ' agora ' had for the Greek. ' Agora ' means the place where people get together ; primarily it means ' gathering ', but this, the normal Homeric use, became

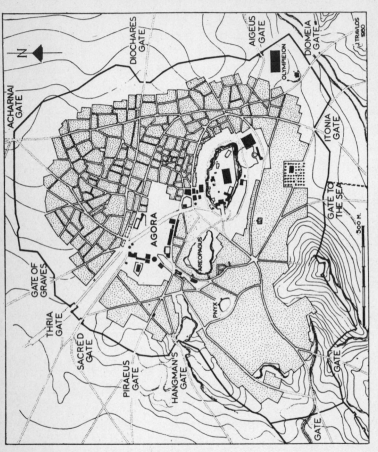

FIG. 1. Athens, fifth century B.C. (Travlos, fig. 20; some streets are known from remains, position of gates, etc. most are restored on probable lines

Map labels: N, ACHARNAI GATE, DIOCHARES GATE, AIGEUS GATE, OLYMPIEION, DIOMEIA GATE, ITONIA GATE, GATE TO THE SEA, 300 M., GATE, GATE, PNYX, AREOPAGUS, AGORA, GATE OF GRAVES, THRIA GATE, SACRED GATE, PIRAEUS GATE, HANGMAN'S GATE, TRAVLOS 1960

subordinate and exceptional in later authors. In the agora the Greeks gathered together for political, commercial or social business. Its natural place, at least in the early phases, was near the acropolis, not far from its main entrance ; such a site was convenient and safe. Thus agora and acropolis formed a sort of double nucleus. With the passage of time and political change the relation between the two became different. In practical and political importance the agora constantly gained at the expense of the acropolis, until in the end it became the most vital and distinctive element of the city. As government evolved from monarchy by way of aristocracy towards democracy — a cycle through which many cities passed — the acropolis was no longer the vital nucleus but an appendage ; though in the process it might even gain in sanctity and venerability, and it could still on occasion serve as a fortress.

In many other ways, too, the gradual emergence of a large body of free and equal citizens, all taking a full and active part in political and social life, guided the architectural growth of the city. The machinery of government became more complicated. Deliberative, legislative and judicial bodies, and magistrates, including those among whom were distributed the powers of the king, became more numerous and acquired new dignity. The corresponding architectural growth was inevitable, but slow and unsystematic and irregular. Various occasions might arise for the erection of new buildings — the proposal of some enterprising person, the accession of new funds, the desire to commemorate a success and use the proceeds of spoils of war ; but the varied and growing needs of the community, which had to be satisfied little by little, provided the real motive. The growth was essentially democratic ; but one must give the ' tyrants ' credit for the important part they played. ' Tyrants ' in the original Greek sense, that is unconstitutional (though not necessarily bad) rulers as opposed to hereditary kings, are constantly cropping up in the course of Greek history. In the seventh and sixth centuries they played a particularly important part. In some cities they held a key-point in political development, providing a necessary transition between aristocracy and democracy ; many of them wisely devoted much thought and money to public works and monuments.

The archaic period in Greece was a time of great commercial expansion too ; this created the need for yet more new buildings and provided the wealth with which to erect them. We shall have occasion to study the whole process in more detail in some later chapters. Only a few cities, however, became really wealthy, and everywhere changing conditions gave rise to intractable political and economic problems. The small resources of the independent city-states set strict limits to the achievements of Greek architecture.

On a higher plane than political and commercial expansion, but by no means detached from it, the temples of the city's gods multiplied and spread and took on a more stately form ; from early archaic times the temple was singled out as the most appropriate medium in which to embody the finest artistic achievements of the city and to express its highest aspirations. The temples were the only buildings in the archaic city with any pretensions to architectural magnificence. Increasingly substantial, beautiful and costly materials were used for them. Unbaked brick and wood gave way to stone ; ultimately marble was used for the finest temples, after a period when its use was mainly confined to decorative sculpture. Stone was expensive to quarry and transport, and the use of fine and carefully worked stone on a large scale continued right through the Hellenic period to be restricted mainly to temples and the more important public buildings. For ordinary purposes sun-dried brick on a stone or rubble foundation still sufficed ; baked brick was known but rarely used, perhaps again for reasons of economy. One must not think of even fifth-century Athens as a city of splendid buildings and gleaming marble ; the nobler monuments stood out against a sober background.

The houses in which the growing population lived were mostly huddled together in irregular groups, between which the narrow streets insinuated themselves. The main streets, leading in from the gates and forming a continuation of the roads outside, converged erratically upon the agora. In so far as the plan of the city had any recognizable structure, this was provided by the agora and the streets radiating from it ; but the radial form would not be very strongly marked, and when ultimately the whole was reduced to a geometric plan by scientific planners, a different principle was adopted.[4] On this loose framework the rest of the city arranged itself informally ; there was little deliberate or far-sighted planning in the old cities. Public buildings — the *bouleuterion* (council-house), the *prytaneion* (town-hall), the *stoas* or colonnades which were used for all kinds of purposes — had no fixed place in the scheme, though they tended to bunch around the agora. The temples were to be found everywhere, though with a certain concentration on the acropolis and again round the agora. The position of the theatre, stadium and gymnasium, when ultimately special places were found for these purposes, was decided by natural features of the ground.

A wall was loosely flung round the whole at a comparatively late stage, when the growth was in some sense complete. In the cities of other countries and other ages the wall has sometimes been a rigid frame into which the rest has had to fit itself. It was quite different in Greece. The wall had to adapt itself to the shape which the city happened to assume, allowance being made for natural contours and defensibility. Circuit walls did not become common till the sixth century, or normal till the fifth. Earlier the acropolis was the strong point and the rest looked to it for protection.

By the sixth century the city was complete in its essentials, though there was plenty of room for architectural development in various directions. The account I have given of its growth and early form depends largely on inference from the later form of towns such as Athens, which were old-fashioned and conservative. Remains of early archaic towns, apart from monumental temples, are mostly fragmentary and obscure, and throw little light on the general form, though they do confirm its irregularity. Tritsch 5 finds in the Cretan Lato an example of an archaic town, with unusually strong Minoan traditions, as is natural in Crete ; it had an agora of interesting form, on a saddle between two citadels, and small houses closely grouped around it, and narrow irregular streets ; but even here there are difficulties of dating.

The scheme I have outlined may be regarded as normal, but it leaves room for other parallel types and for endless

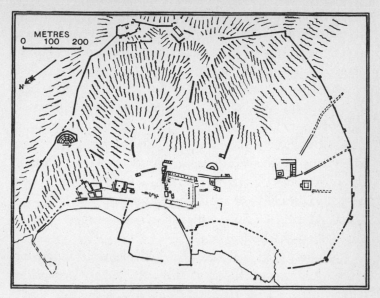

FIG. 2. Thasos (after *B.C.H.* lii, plan facing p. 493).

variation. There was usually something highly individual about each of the older Greek cities in architectural form as in general culture. Then again there were special classes such as the hill towns, built on a plateau, the whole town being an acropolis, though possibly acquiring a lower extension. Keats has the right idea — 'by river or sea-shore or mountain built with peaceful citadel'; though one may query the word 'peaceful'. As for its rivers, Greece had no Thames or Seine or Danube to dominate the form and life of her greatest cities. There were coastal towns, especially among the colonies and newer towns, sometimes built on a peninsula, from which they might ultimately venture to extend to the mainland ; often with the agora near the harbour and the rest of the town in a rough semicircle around it, giving an impressive theatre-like effect on some sites. Some of the oldest towns grew around an acropolis several miles inland, where they were safe from piratical raids ; commerce did not matter so much in the early days ; later, when the need for a good port was imperative, the nearest suitable point on the coast was developed as a harbour town, and if this flourished it might become a sort of duplicate city. The final stage was to join the two towns by fortifications, to ensure supplies by sea if the country were overrun ; Athens set the fashion in this towards the middle of the fifth century and was followed by several others. So we get the scheme : upper city — long walls — harbour town.

It is not a particular position or shape or arrangement which gives the Greek city its character, but the possession of certain essentially Hellenic elements. Most important of all was the agora. The acropolis became superfluous, a survival — though we must remember that one of the things which gave Greek life its peculiar richness was the retention and transformation of archaic survivals. Concentration and coherence about the vital centre, the agora, was invariable. Beyond this we get that endless local and individual variety which makes Hellenic culture so fascinating.

A further word of warning is necessary before going on to the subject of systematic town-planning. One should not get the idea that Greek culture was primarily and almost exclusively urban. The life of the Greek city-state was founded upon agriculture and remained dependent on it. The cultivation of its patch of fertile land, the growing of corn, olives or vines, was important to each city, even the most highly developed, even to those which imported a large part of their food from distant lands. Thucydides tells us that the majority of the Athenians in the fifth century lived normally in the country (ii. 14. 2), and Aristophanes in the *Acharnians* and elsewhere gives vivid glimpses of the deep attachment of a large section of the Athenians to the soil of Attica. There *was* an essentially urban population at Athens (and even more at Peiraeus) as in other large towns, engaged in commerce and industries such as pottery and metal-work, but it was only one element, and not so divorced from the land as the great urban masses of today. In some secluded and backward parts of Greece, urban culture had never developed very highly and men still lived a comparatively primitive life in simple communities (Thucydides i. 5) ; elsewhere a local country deme or parish might retain a vigorous life of its own, though part of a city-state, being in fact an embryo polis which happened not to have grown. City-state and city were not necessarily the same, even though the former was most visibly embodied in the latter. With this caution we may turn again to the city in the narrower sense, which, after all, is what matters most architecturally, though shrines and temples and other buildings are found scattered about the land.

A word about population will be relevant to both old and new cities. The evidence on which attempts have been made to calculate the population of the city-states is hopelessly fragmentary and obscure, and there is the further difficulty of estimating what proportion lived in the urban centre. But it is clear that most Greek cities were small by modern standards. The evidence for Athens is a little more plentiful than most ; [6] Attica may have had in Pericles' time 40,000 citizens and a total free population of about 150,000, of whom less than half lived in the city and its port ; to these may probably be added over 20,000 aliens resident at Athens or Peiraeus for purposes of trade, and over 100,000 slaves. But very few others were on anything approaching this scale. Hardly more than a score of city-states ever had more than 10,000 citizens, *i.e*, a free population of 40,000 or more, and most must have had considerably less. The ideas of thinkers and planners are significant, since they probably reflect the actual state of affairs. Hippodamus thought 10,000 the right number (Aristotle, *Politics* ii. 5. 2 ; it is not clear whether he meant citizens or inhabitants — I imagine the former). Plato (*Laws* v. 737 E) mentions 5040 'sharers in the land' as a typical figure, though the number will depend on the size of the territory. Aristotle is cautious in the matter of statistics ; 'Ten people would not make a city', he says (*Nic. Ethics* ix. 10. 3, Rackham's translation), 'and with a hundred thousand it is a city no longer'; but the general principles which he gives in the *Politics* (vii. 4) go to the heart of the matter. The polis must have a population which is 'self-sufficient for the purpose of living the good life after the manner of a political community'; but it must not be so unwieldy that the members cannot maintain personal contact with one another — 'in order to decide questions of justice and in order to distribute the offices according to merit it is necessary for the citizens to know each other's personal characters' (Rackham).

II

GREEK TOWN-PLANNING [1]

IN the sixth and fifth centuries, when Hellenic civilization was well advanced and the architectural growth
of the city-state pretty well complete, the Greeks were
still frequently creating new cities — colonies, capitals for
federal states and leagues, and replacements of towns very
thoroughly destroyed by the Persians and others. In
such circumstances it would have been surprising if the
inventive genius of the Greeks had not produced some
way of town-planning, and attempted to create a city
deliberately instead of simply letting it grow ; and in
fact by the fifth century practical needs had suggested
methods, and at the same time architects had had visions
of an ideal architectural form for the polis, and were
attempting to put them into practice, though aesthetic
theory was never allowed to predominate.

We have no means of knowing how the new methods
came into being and were first applied, but there can be
little doubt that their home was Ionia on the west coast
of Asia Minor, and probably Miletus in particular. There
is little sign of planning in the western colonies until
comparatively late, and the cities of Greece proper
remained obstinately conservative in form. The archaic
Ionians took the cultural lead in various directions, and
in this matter in particular they had good opportunities
for experiment, through colonization and through the
need for rebuilding cities which had been razed. One

might add that Ionia was particularly susceptible to Eastern influences, but I doubt whether this accounted for much in town-planning, even though analogies can be found in Egypt and the East. It is an injustice to the native intelligence of the Greeks to attach too much importance to external models and teachers and influences. A safer assumption is that Ionian architects worked out independently a system which would satisfy their own needs and their own idea of what a city should be. The basic principle was nothing outlandish or elaborate, but a simple, obvious and practical one. It was in fact the most elementary of plans, the so-called ' gridiron ' or ' chess-board ', with straight streets crossing at right angles.

No great genius was needed to think out this method. Groups of colonists were constantly being confronted, after hitting on their site, with the problem how to divide up the ground most easily and conveniently and to the greatest general satisfaction. The rectangular method meant the least complications. Where real ingenuity was shown was in adapting the Greek city, with all its old original elements, to this rigid frame, and in making the most of the architectural possibilities which the process of adaptation offered. The chess-board plan is looked at askance by many modern planners, especially if applied rigidly on a large scale ; it is unimaginative and inelastic. But the objections do not apply so strongly in the case of the Greek cities. They were comparatively small and had not to contend with the problems of traffic and so forth which arise in a great modern city. They could not afford to spread themselves. The ' gridiron ' served their purposes well enough. They made no pretence of aiming at grandiose or picturesque effects, splendid vistas and the like. But for all that, with a little ingenuity, especially in the siting and arrangement of buildings, they could avoid formless monotony and bring off a successful scheme.

Miletus apparently played an important part. After sending out an incredible number of colonies, the mother-city was destroyed by the Persians in 494 B.C., and re-founded on modern lines after the defeat of the Persians in 479 B.C. ; and the most famous personality in Greek town-planning, Hippodamus, was a Milesian. This Hippodamus is an elusive figure. Our most important source for him is Aristotle (*Politics* ii. 5) ; we are told here that he had long hair and held interesting political theories, but of his activities as a planner merely that he ' discovered the method of dividing cities and cut up Peiraeus ' ; and other references are not much more precise. We can be sure that he planned Peiraeus for the Athenians, towards the middle of the fifth century. We are told that he took part in the colonization of Thurii in south Italy (443 B.C.) and one cannot doubt that he had a hand in planning the new town. Strabo speaks of his having planned Rhodes (founded 408 B.C.) (xiv. 2. 9), but adds doubtfully ' as they say '. It is unlikely that this last tradition is true ; it makes him incredibly young when he carried out his work at Peiraeus, or else incredibly old when he planned Rhodes. Von Gerkan is probably right [2] in pushing his boyhood back into the sixth century and assuming that as a young man he had experience at the rebuilding of his own city before he brought the new ideas to Athens. We cannot doubt that he used the rectangular plan ; Aristotle (*Politics* vii. 10. 4, 1330 b) implies but does not prove it. Attempts have been made in the past to attribute to him radial planning and other spectacular devices, but the evidence for this is imaginary, and it is reasonable to suppose that the methods which seem to have been normal in his own time and the fourth century were those of the most notable exponent of Greek town-planning. Not that he invented them or was the first to use them in Greece — more probably he developed them and made them more widely known. When we read of his ' invention ' we must remember that the Greeks were notoriously fond of transforming what was in fact a slow development, to which many contributed, into the more spectacular creation of one man. References to his ' allocation ' of ground may point to the fact that he showed real ingenuity in arranging his cities and allotting sections for different purposes. But in spite of the assumptions which we may make with due caution, Hippodamus remains little more than a name to us ; a convenient name, however, and I shall feel justified in labelling the Greek method Hippodamian.

We know little about the earliest planned towns, with the exception of Miletus, and again have to supplement the scanty evidence with inferences from later phases. Olbia, a colony of Miletus on the northern shore of the Euxine, was rebuilt after a fire at the end of the sixth century ; the excavations show that it was given a rectangular street plan, but the details of this are not clear. Miletus was a very ancient city, and in its archaic form was irregularly built, as far as can be judged from the slight remains of the period. The Persian sack was very thorough, and the returning Milesian survivors planned an entirely new and modern city, unlike the Athenians, who also returned to find their city destroyed, but gradually restored the *status quo ante*, with the addition of more magnificent temples. The new plan with its rectangular network of streets seems to have involved the whole of the Milesian peninsula, save that the southern part, where the orientation is very slightly different and the blocks larger, may be a somewhat later extension. Much less would be required immediately, and actual building would proceed slowly as prosperity gradually returned. The Milesians seem to have had visions of their city regaining much of its former greatness, and to have planned accordingly. It was a great work and it was justified ; Miletus became a flourishing city again, though its archaic cultural eminence was gone for ever. The orientation was chosen with care and skill, so that one set of streets ran along the length of the peninsula. An extensive central area, comparatively low-lying and flat, was reserved from the first for development as agora — there is no sign of houses having to be cleared away for the great architectural schemes carried out later. The factors which determined the position of the agora were mainly the same as those which had operated from the earliest times, but the principles involved could be more deliberately applied, and provision could be made for future growth. Ingenuity was shown in fitting theatre, stadium, gymnasia and such buildings into the plan, as we shall see in later chapters.

Outside Ionia, their district of origin, the new methods were for some time applied only very sporadically ; this is particularly true of Greece proper. Elis, for instance, newly founded by synoecism in 471 B.C., was still old-fashioned. Hippodamus came to Athens at a time when the city was beginning to attract many of the intellectual

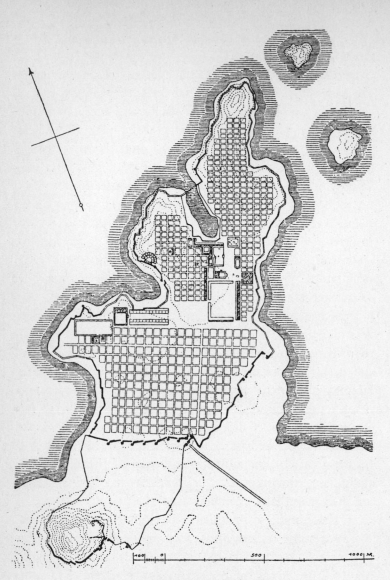

FIG. 3. Miletus (von Gerkan, Taf. 6)

leaders of Greece. We know hardly anything of his plan for Peiraeus. Modern reconstructions of it are mainly works of imagination. The hills and harbours offered a difficult broken site, and there is some slight indication that the rectangular scheme was used with different orientation in different quarters.[3] The ' gridiron ' was imposed on hilly sites for which a modern planner would probably think it most inappropriate, but this does not mean that practical convenience was pedantically sacrificed to abstract theory. Provided that there were several fairly level main streets, that was sufficient for the traffic of a Greek town ; many of the minor cross-streets might be little more than stairways. The agora at Peiraeus, placed in a depression west of the hill Munychia, was called Hippodameia after the planner, who presumably provided a place for it in his ' division ' of the site.

Of Thurii we are merely told, by Diodorus (xii. 10), that there were three streets one way, four the other ; this is a very small number, and there may have been alleys between, though von Gerkan (p. 57) thinks such an arrangement unlikely. At Olynthus in Chalcidike, north of the Aegean (p. 187 below), the older part of the town, on the south hill, was irregular ; but in the latter part of the fifth century the north hill, which was lower and less steep, was laid out in rectangular fashion, with several long avenues running north and south along the ridge, and numerous cross streets alternating with narrow alleys which bisected the blocks. The same system was extended for some distance over the lower ground east of both hills, though the cross streets were not actually carried down the east slope. There were some departures from the rectangular, round the edge of the hill, for

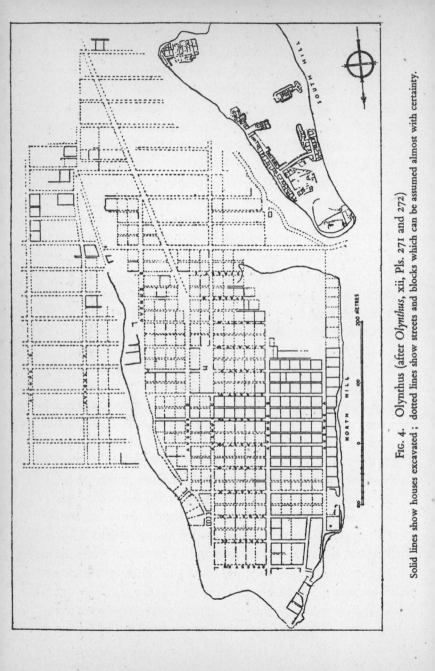

FIG. 4. Olynthus (after *Olynthus*, xii, Pls. 271 and 272)

Solid lines show houses excavated; dotted lines show streets and blocks which can be assumed almost with certainty.

example, and where one of the 'avenues' is thought to have struck off diagonally south-eastwards towards the harbour town of Mecyberna. The south hill had an 'East Side Avenue' and a 'West Side Avenue', joined by cross streets; so that the new plan of the north quarter represented the reduction to a set scheme of the old plan of the south. Selinus too, in western Sicily, was built on two flattish hills, but had a curiously different history. The south hill, overlooking the harbour which was formed by an arm of the sea to the east, was the oldest part; but at an early date the city expanded on to a larger hill to the north, as well as on to the low ground east and west; the south hill became a sort of acropolis, and on it was built a series of fine temples. Selinus was sacked by the Carthaginians in 409. Shortly afterwards it was restored, but now it was confined to the south hill again, where it was laid out on rectangular lines. The main street ran north to south from end to end of the hill, and there were a number of cross-streets, of which one, running across the widest part of the pear-shaped hill, forms an emphatic transverse axis. Two points deserve special notice. The old temples still figure largely and occupy a rather disproportionate amount of space in the south-eastern quarter; indeed the orientation and the line of the main streets seem to have been deter-mined by them. Secondly, the cross formation of the main streets is more marked than is usual in Greek plan-ning and is like the Italian scheme of *cardo* and *decumanus*. Over-confident and fanciful restorations of Selinus have been made in the past.

Rhodes, founded 408 B.C., was compared admiringly to a great theatre (Vitruvius ii. 8. 11, says something

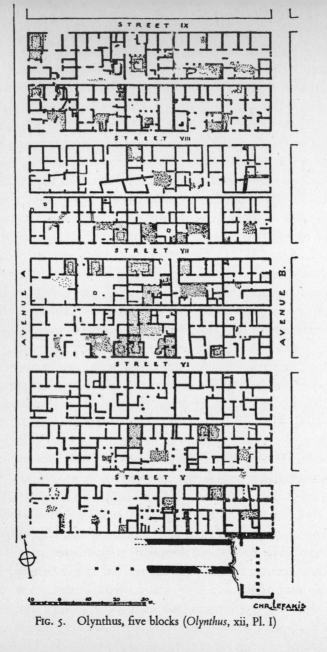

FIG. 5. Olynthus, five blocks (*Olynthus*, xii, Pl. I)

similar of Halicarnassus, laid out by Mausollus towards the middle of the fourth century). This, as we have seen, was a form which a seaside town might naturally tend to take. The simile may merely be suggested by the contours of the site and the outline of the city. There is no need to press it further and assume that the main streets radiated from the agora as the gangways of a theatre from the orchestra. In fact Greek planning showed little tendency towards radial treatment till late. Cnidos in south-west Asia Minor was another coastal town in the same region. It was originally on a small peninsula, but after the Persian Wars it was in the end restored chiefly on the adjoining mainland. The site sloped steeply, and while the long streets ran more or less level, parallel with the sea coast, the cross-streets climbed steeply and were provided with steps. A shifting of the site of a city, or at least of its centre of gravity, was not uncommon in Asia, though rare in Greece proper.

On some sites the evidence is scanty or obscure, complicated by later accretions or confused by the hasty assumptions of early investigators. Priene still provides our clearest object-lesson in Hippodamian town-planning. When we come to examine various elements in detail, Priene will furnish excellent examples at almost every point. On a small scale it is a model Greek city, containing everything which makes a polis, all very neatly and ingeniously arranged and subordinated to the Hippodamian plan. The city was refounded in the latter part of the fourth century. It was built on the southern slope of a hill, and again the long east-to-west streets were comparatively level while the cross-streets were steep. A much steeper, in fact almost inaccessible, area to the north

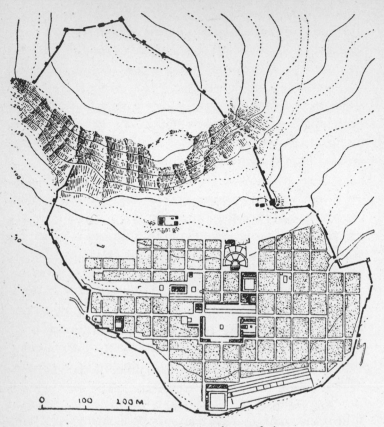

FIG. 6. Priene (von Gerkan, Taf. 9)

was included and formed a kind of acropolis, and the wall was flung very loosely and irregularly around the whole. The rectangular plan was strictly applied to house-blocks and public places and buildings, and only a few minor deviations were allowed. A convenient central area, tangential to the most important of the long east-to-west streets, was reserved for the agora. Some of the temples and public buildings were effectively placed.

26

The fine temple of Athena stood in a commanding position on a terrace north-west of the agora ; the theatre at the top of the built-up area balanced a gymnasium with stadium attached at the bottom. Priene can only have had a population of about 4000, but we must not let our natural interest in the great and famous cities of Greece make us forget that there were few like Corinth, hardly any like Athens, but hundreds like Priene in size, and they all rightly claimed the name polis.

From the time of Priene onwards Hippodamian methods were more extensively used, particularly in Asia in the numerous foundations of Alexander the Great and his successors (Dura-Europos is a good example). In the Hellenistic age the cities no longer enjoyed that lively independence with which their greatest deeds were identified ; but often they had considerable local autonomy, not to speak of benevolent royal patronage, and the form of the Greek city lived on, and indeed grew in some ways and multiplied. More specifically Hellenistic achievements, such as the spectacular creations of the architects of Pergamon in north-west Asia Minor, are outside our present province, though I shall sometimes have occasion to refer to them by way of contrast. One could hardly have a stronger contrast than between Priene and Pergamon, for instance. Pergamon, as developed by its kings in the third and second centuries B.C., was a thoroughly Hellenistic city, as opposed to the Hellenic cities with which we are mainly concerned. T. Fyfe [4] calls Pergamon the work of a *real* planner, apparently in contrast with the Hippodamian towns. But that is unfair to the latter. The upper town of Pergamon, with its crescent of great buildings on the crest of the hill and the

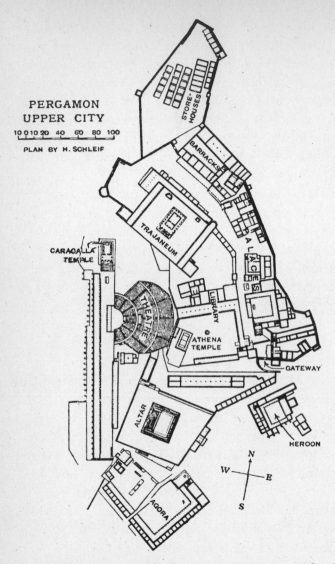

PERGAMON
UPPER CITY

10 0 10 20 40 60 80 100

PLAN BY H. SCHLEIF

STORE-HOUSES

BARRACKS

TRAJANEUM

CARACALLA
TEMPLE

THEATRE

PALACES

LIBRARY

ATHENA
TEMPLE

GATEWAY

ALTAR

HEROON

N
W — E
S

AGORA

FIG. 7. Pergamon, upper city (Pauly-Wissowa, xix. 1, p. 1235, fig. 3)

theatre skilfully inserted in the slope, was certainly magnificent. But there was something extravagant about it, a spirit akin to the sculpture of the great altar of Pergamon ; the kings and their architects were showing what they could do, with resources surpassing those of even a prosperous Hellenic city. The builders of Priene were providing the essentials of a small Greek city-state. Miletus and Priene need not fear comparison.

When we come to consider general principles we find that they were few and simple. Greek town-planning was the very opposite of academic, and as far as we can tell there was no recognized body of theory. Plato (*Laws* 778, 9) and Aristotle (*Politics* vii. 10. 11) in prescribing the proper form of a city confine themselves to the most general recommendations. ' The difficulty with such things is not so much in the matter of theory but in that of practice ', says Aristotle ; each architect or planner had to use his ingenuity in coping with the problems of each particular site. Careful planning was by the fourth century recognized as a good thing and an asset to a city ; the chaotic state of the streets of Athens was condemned by some writers. Aristotle (vii. 10. 4) approves of the ' modern, Hippodamian fashion ', with the reservation that a city will be more secure against enemy penetration if certain parts deviate from the regular.

Nor was the primary object of Hippodamian planning aesthetic, though the architects, like all Greek artists, unerringly seized upon the opportunity offered for the creation of new beauty. The motive in the first place was provided by the practical needs of the colonies, as we have seen ; the Greek instinct for orderliness and harmony also came into play, and admittedly this was closely bound up with their sense of beauty. But the whole thing was a reduction to order of elements already in existence ; no sacrifice was made of these and no violence done to them. Hippodamus has sometimes been called the ancient Haussmann ; this gives quite a wrong impression. 'Haussmannization', if I understand the term rightly, means the arbitrary imposition of a bold and masterful design ; broad straight streets are driven ruthlessly through the city ; the result may be architecturally magnificent in itself, but it is apt to be a little overpowering, a little inorganic in its relation to the previous state of affairs and to the rest of the city. Hippodamian planning is less ambitious. Besides being used mainly on new sites and not forced on already existing towns, it produced no such startling effect on the appearance of the city. The change, I fancy, would be less obvious in the actual streets of a city than it is in a plan on paper. Still less did it betoken an inner or spiritual change. 'The difference between regular and irregular, " Hippodamian " and archaic Greek towns', says Tritsch,[5] ' is a purely formal and external one.' Both alike can be called polis. All the vital elements are still there in the new towns, standing in the same general relation to one another. The process was essentially a tidying-up, not a revolution. Of course even within these limitations the development was highly important in itself, and produced important incidental results, some of which we shall examine. Certain of the old original elements underwent interesting changes in the process of being fitted in ; rectangular planning gave an impulse towards the creation of more finished architectural types.

Above all, if a city was planned from the beginning on Hippodamian lines, that is, if besides the rectangular street system being plotted out, sites were allotted in advance for the various purposes, the development which had formerly been haphazard and partly unconscious could now be carefully controlled and subordinated to a fixed design, though it was not necessarily much more rapid. An inscription of Colophon in Asia Minor (see p. 192 below) shows how the citizens, when extending and rebuilding their city at the end of the fourth century, resolved to appoint a committee of ten whose duty would be to plan the line of the walls and secure the services of the best available architect to lay out the roads and assign building lots, reserving suitable places for the agora and public buildings. (But first of all vows were made to the gods to hold a procession and sacrifice when the work was done.)

Hippocrates (*Airs, Waters and Places* iii-vi) thinks an eastward aspect healthiest for a city; Aristotle too (*Politics* vii. 10. 1) thinks that a city should be on a slope facing east, or failing that, south. Neither prescribes any particular orientation for the street system. Certain authors had peculiar ideas about so orientating the streets as to admit or exclude certain winds (see Vitruvius i. 6); to make these work, the winds would have to cooperate by always blowing along certain fixed lines. In practice there seem to have been no fixed rules or principles, and endless variety, with a preference, where convenient, for N.-S. and E.-W. The contours were the decisive factor. On level ground the choice was free. On a slope or a ridge the long main streets naturally ran with the contours as far as possible, the cross-streets took the steeper course.

Once selected, the orientation was strictly but not pedantic-ally maintained ; particular deviations were allowed at awkward points ; rarely, as far as we can tell, did different quarters have different orientations. There is little evidence for religious influence in this matter, save that the favourite E.–W. N.–S. arrangement allowed the temples to have their traditional orientation, facing east.

Apart from being straight and parallel, the streets were not so very different from what they had always been. On the whole they tended to be a little wider than in the old-fashioned towns, but still not what we should call wide.[6] Four, five or six yards were common widths ; in most towns several important streets were given a little more, and we hear of exceptional streets two or three times as wide. But as far as evidence goes, there was little tendency towards really spacious street-planning, or towards a more impressive architectural treatment. Long colonnaded streets and fine vistas do not come till late Hellenistic or Roman times. The crossing of two main streets is seldom if ever the basis of the plan. ' The Greek city street', says von Gerkan (p. 84), ' cannot be con-sidered a dominant element in the design, giving in its own right a monumental impression ; rather even the main streets arise out of natural needs, to provide room for the increased traffic around the market and the centre of government.' The surface was still merely hard earth as a rule ; paving was only added in particular places for special reasons — for example, on steep ground to prevent rain water washing the street away. Some of the long avenues at Olynthus were paved with cobbles. The more systematic paving of streets belongs mainly to Roman times. Drains, both open and covered, were rather more freely provided than before, but were still very inadequate. Raised side-walks were rare.

The agora was still the core of the whole structure, giving it coherence, and the great centre of city life. A number of rectangular blocks in the middle were reserved for it, and the architectural treatment which was devised for it in the fourth century and early Hellenistic times is perhaps the most interesting by-product of Hippodamian planning. The shrines are still scattered about the city, with the difference that they can now be neatly accommodated, each in a block or two. Residential quarters fill in what is left over. And still the wall is draped very loosely around, seeking a defensible line more persistently than ever, since in the fourth century siege-craft made great strides. The wall was almost entirely independent of the street system ; the main gates normally, but by no means always, opened on to an important street, but they were not placed in its axis if by a different orientation they could be made stronger. The acropolis had become largely superfluous in the old towns, and it could be dispensed with in the new unless it happened that a dominating height could conveniently be taken in by the fortifications.

Literary references and remains alike justify us in regarding the system of straight streets at right angles as *the* Greek method *par excellence*. But even after it was well established it was far from dominating the Greek world. The old cities of Greece proper, in particular, obstinately clung to their old form. It was quite impracticable, even if the will had been there, to replan thoroughly a city whose existence on the same site continued unbroken. This kind of thing can only be achieved by a very far-sighted plan, extending over a great many years, and coordinated even though carried out piecemeal. Such a plan was hardly to be expected of an old Greek city, though on new sites extraordinary foresight was shown in providing for development which would probably go on into the distant future. The alternative was wholesale removal to another site ; this was a frequent occurrence among the Asiatic cities, but the cities of European Greece could hardly bring themselves to it, even though the old site, chosen for security rather than convenience, might have been abandoned with advantage. Particular sections might be given a more regular modernized form (the agora of Athens for instance), though not necessarily on strictly rectangular lines ; but there is little evidence for Haussmannization or any form of drastic modernization of the old cities. Even where a city was razed to the ground, it tended to resume something not unlike its original form, on its original site, in old Greece. Thebes, however, after its complete destruction by Alexander the Great, was regularly planned, mainly confined now to its old citadel, the Cadmea. Another sign of the limited application of the Hippodamian method is that new cities continued to be built on less regular lines. This was so in the case of Elis (471 B.C.). Megalopolis, founded about 371 B.C., was architecturally ambitious but not Hippodamian in design, as far as we can tell ; nor was Mantinea, rebuilt about the same time after the interesting but trying experience of being split up by the jealous Spartans into the original constituent villages out of which it had been formed by synoecism in the previous century. Finally we have seen how, in the course of the

Hellenistic age, more grandiose architectural conceptions emerged, particularly at Pergamon and in its sphere of influence, where fine effects were achieved by a bold use of terracing. On the other hand, in the mass-production of new Hellenistic cities in Asia which took place under Alexander and his successors, the chess-board plan was normal, with a certain uniformity and standardization — in such matters as the proportions of the blocks — which was foreign to the earlier period.

III

FORTIFICATIONS [1]

ABOUT the acropolis very little needs to be added. It was once the city's main bulwark, augmented at most by outworks of moderate size extending over the lower ground. In the fully developed city its rôle was more restricted, and it formed a great redoubt in the city wall, or less commonly an inner keep. The circuit walls were now the city's great defence, and no pains were spared to make them impregnable ; they were no mere first line ; with them the city stood or fell. When this phase was reached, an acropolis could be dispensed with ; we hear (*e.g.* Pausanias viii. 8. 4, 12. 7 — Mantinea) of cities abandoning their primitive site, with its acropolis, for one more convenient. Some later towns such as Priene and Heraclea (Latmos) possessed a sort of acropolis almost by accident — an outlying piece of high ground taken in by the walls for reasons of strength and not necessarily fortified on the side of the town. New Miletus at first included in its walls the hill on the south which was the nucleus of the old town, but later abandoned it, a cross-wall being built in the lower ground (see fig. 3). The size of the acropolis varied greatly from a small bastion to a vast circuit like the Acrocorinthus.

Dealing with fortifications, Aristotle says (*Politics* vii. 10. 4), 'An acropolis is suitable for oligarchy and monarchy, level ground for democracy'. For kings, oligarchies and tyrants the acropolis was enough ; on occasion it could provide protection against disaffection within the city as well as danger without. Under democracy strong protection was sought for the whole community ; and in fact separate fortification and armed occupation of the acropolis was felt to be anti-democratic and a symbol of tyranny — or else of foreign domination. Strong walls were a sign of a sturdy and defiant autonomy ; when a city was defeated and surrendered its independence, the victors sometimes demanded the demolition of the outer walls and themselves placed a garrison in the acropolis.

In spite of these limitations, the acropolis still counted for a great deal in the life of many of the older cities, because of the sanctity of its shrines and because of the traditions which clung to it. G. Fougères emphasizes the antithesis between agora and acropolis ; ' Below, was the buzz (*bourdonnement*) ', he says, ' of the life of labour, business, industry and politics ; above, the serenity of a supra-terrestrial atmosphere, where the gods reign alone among the smoke of sacrifices and the murmur of prayers ; while a handful of soldiers scan the horizon from the height of the ramparts '.[2] There is some slight exaggeration in this contrast, as we shall see when we come to the agora. Religion and art being inseparably bound together, the finest gems of sculpture and architecture were often to be found on the acropolis. The brilliant development of the Acropolis of Athens was exceptional only in degree, not in kind.

The circuit walls hang on to the acropolis, even though it represents the beginnings and they are a later addition. They are among the Greek cities' most impressive monuments. On many sites, where now hardly anything else is to be seen, the walls still stand to a considerable height and create a deep impression of grandeur and beauty. As feats of engineering they are not surpassed in the whole range of Greek architecture ; and the construction of a powerful wall several miles in length was the most laborious and expensive task with which a city was faced. Though austerely practical they could still often be reckoned among the city's architectural glories. Aristotle says (*Politics* vii. 10. 8) that the wall ought to be an ornament as well as a protection. It would be the first thing to impress a visitor, and it was meant to have a depressing effect on an approaching enemy.

Apart from the grandeur of the whole circuit and the massive and simple beauty of the gates and towers, Greek walls have the peculiar charm of well-designed masonry wrought with great skill and care. They provide striking examples of the genius of the Greeks for combining the useful and the beautiful. Fine masonry is found in many other structures too, but it can best be appreciated in walls which stand in their own right. Greek masonry is genuine ; its appearance is seldom false to its real nature and inner structure. Fortification walls many feet thick with rubble cores are no exception ; their construction merely shows a natural and obvious economy ; and the large well-fitted blocks with which they are faced are no veneer but a massive part of the whole, penetrating deep and giving added strength. The Hellenic architects had a great tradition in their land to inspire them in wall building ; the magnificent Cyclopean and ashlar masonry of Mycenean fortresses would still be visible in some places ; in fact they were sometimes patched up and used.

In both ages the great walls seem to grow from the rock and to belong inseparably to the landscape.

However important it was in the end, the fortification wall was not a primary or essential element in the architectural form of the city. Historically it was a late addition ; some towns remained unwalled in classical times, Sparta and Elis for example. A city could be a complete Greek city without a wall ; it could *not* be without an agora, or a gymnasium or theatre. Plato in the *Laws* (778 D) makes a speaker say that it is best to leave the walls ' lying asleep in the earth ' ; the swords of the citizens are the only true bulwark ; brave men should meet the enemy on the frontiers ; walls are a temptation to cowards to give ground without a fight. But most people, including Aristotle, took the common-sense view that it was best even for brave men to have a fortified base of operations.

The wall was loosely flung around the city ; it was not the frame into which the rest was fitted, and it was not normally a dominant factor in the plan. This is particularly true of the earlier towns ; in those which were founded comparatively late, when walls had become usual and were considered a necessity, a circuit might be marked out and built up at an early phase, for the sake of immediate security ; but still the outline was irregular and did not conform to a type. In the comparatively minor rôle played by the walls in the structure of the city one may contrast Greece with Egypt and the East, and with Italy too. Italian town-planning had strong military and religious associations ; the town was related to the camp, in which a rectangular *vallum* with its gates placed in the axis of the two main streets defined the whole plan and fixed the type.

The building of city walls probably began in Ionia, whose cities had to face the threat of attack from a series of much more powerful enemies. The European mother- land followed suit somewhat later. Probably in early archaic times the fortification of the whole town was exceptional, though it is difficult to decide this question, since early walls of simple construction, unbaked brick on a low rubble socle, may have disappeared and left no trace. The practice became comparatively common in the course of the sixth century and normal in the fifth ; but there are notable exceptions. Sparta, while her military supremacy lasted, could dispense with fortifica- tions ; Elis, newly founded in the fifth century, was not given a wall. Whether Athens was fully walled before the Persian Wars is a question hotly disputed by archaeologists.[3]

In planning the circuit the architects would have to strike a balance between economy and strength. The transport of stone was particularly expensive. Labour and material had to be conserved, and this could best be done by taking the shortest line which would enclose the built-up area ; but a diversion often meant a more defensible line. On flat ground no complications arose, and the wall would approximate to a circle (as at Man- tinea), the figure whose circumference is least in proportion to its area. But almost always there were unusual factors ; in particular, on most sites there were irregularities of ground offering possibilities of defence ; and often the city wall wandered considerably from its shortest possible line in search of contours which would give natural strength, so that fewer men would be required for manning in spite of the added length. Walls followed the crest of a ridge or ran a little below it on the slope facing the enemy, so that they were conveniently lower inside than out. On very precipitous ground a stretch of wall could sometimes be safely omitted altogether. On the other hand, strategic extensions often involved great engineering difficulties, and the architects acquired amazing skill in overcoming these. Good defensibility was more and more necessary as, from the end of the fifth century onwards, the science of siege-craft advanced ; however inconvenient it was, the wall had to take such a line that the formidable siege-engines could not easily be brought to bear and vulnerable points were well covered. Syracuse provides a striking example. The plateau of Epipolae, stretching over two miles to the westward, proved a powerful threat to the city when occupied by an enemy force. In the fourth century it was included in the fortifications, though the resulting wall was of enormous length and enclosed a great extent of ground not otherwise needed. Because of these requirements, and because the cities they enclosed were built to no standard form, Greek walls show great variety of plan. The length, too, varied very widely, and was by no means in proportion to population or area enclosed. Syracuse with about seventeen miles was freakish, but five, six or seven miles was not out of the ordinary for the larger cities, and ' long walls ' to the sea meant a big addition.

Subsidiary structures were confined to the essentials — gates and towers. The curtain walls in between were provided with parapets and battlements, and at Athens, according to an inscription,[4] with an ingeniously constructed covered gallery on top. Parapets had to be made increasingly solid when in the fourth century artillery was produced which was capable of flattening them and robbing the defenders of their ' cover '. The towers were placed at commanding points, at intervals which vary greatly according to the requirements of the defence. They are sometimes bonded into the wall, sometimes not, and often they are of superior masonry, more massive and regular. They are more often square than round, and vary from mere bulges on the face of the wall to great roomy structures. Some of them had only one fighting platform, with no roof above, but more often there was an upper storey, or even several, and doors opened from the first floor on to the wall-top. Sometimes the ground floor consisted not of a room but a rubble-filled base for the upper storeys. Loop-holes or archer-slots were, of course, provided. The defence was concentrated in the towers. Their main object was to enable the defenders to bring enfilading fire to bear on the attackers. This could be done without towers in some sections where angles and salients made it possible ; and a simple and primitive method of enfilading was the ' indented trace ', a series of kinks or serrations produced by making short sections of wall run at right angles to the general line.[5] This method was used in archaic fortifications, but was superseded by the tower in the fifth and fourth centuries, though it reappears later in combination with towers. Occasionally gates too were placed at right angles to the line of the wall, by means of a kink and an overlap. The gates were simple in design, without superfluous ornament. Important gates were flanked by towers ; there were also small and inconspicuous posterns. Sometimes there was an inner

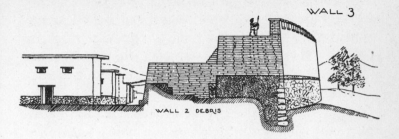

FIG. 8. Smyra, restored section of archaic wall (R. V. Nicholls, *Annual of British School at Athens*, liii–liv, p. 51, fig. 7) 1958–59

and an outer gate, with a small circular or rectangular courtyard between ; this scheme had the advantage that if the attackers broke through the outer gate they would still not be inside the city and in fact would be particularly vulnerable ; indeed, in the Isthmian Gate at Corinth and others there was no provision for closing the outer opening, and the whole arrangement was in the nature of a trap. Arched gateways began to be used in Hellenistic times. A certain sanctity naturally belonged to the city gates, and votive niches and even small shrines are sometimes found in them.

More elaborate defensive and counter-offensive arrangements are rare. A couple of specimens from Sicily are more reminiscent of mediaeval military architecture than ancient Greek.[6] The vulnerable western tip of Epipolae at Syracuse was defended by an elaborate system of ditches, massive towers for mounting artillery, and passages for internal communication and sallies against the enemy. A similar fortress guarding the northern tip of the acropolis at Selinus seems to show the same cunning hand, which may be that of Dionysius, tyrant of Syracuse early in the fourth century B.C., and a master of the science of warfare. But such methods did not spread ; in general a comparatively simple system of towers and curtain walls and tower-flanked gates proved sufficient, if skilfully planned.

The walls were the city's last line of defence, unless a desperate stand was made on the acropolis. Its first line was the mountain barrier which the enemy usually had to cross. Sometimes rough walls were built to block the passes ; or fortresses were placed on dominant heights. The border forts of Attica have left remains which are among the finest examples of ancient fortification. Even simple watch-towers, which completed the system, were sometimes built of first-class masonry.

The method of construction of fortification walls is very varied. The best of all (Messene for example) were built in their full height and thickness of large blocks of the finest masonry, carefully wrought and fitted, without binding material or even clamps ; [7] but such an expensive and laborious method was not in general use. More often the fitted blocks were merely a very substantial facing on either side of a rubble core or other rough filling,[8] and their own inner faces were left irregular ; or only the foundations and socle were of stone, and the upper structure of unbaked brick — a material which can be made far more durable and strong than is often imagined ; in fact Pausanias says that it withstands siege-engines better than stone (viii. 8. 7, on Mantinea, where the walls were of this construction). The thickness

FIG. 9.   Heraclea (Latmos), restoration of wall (*Milet*, iii. 2, Abb. 17)

ranged from about six feet to thirteen or more, and was apt to vary even in the same wall.

NOTE ON TECHNIQUE

To attempt a full account of technique would be out of place in this work ; but since to a much greater extent than in other structures the appearance and the whole architectural character of these walls depends on the style of the masonry, I should like to develop the subject in a short appendix, in order to do full justice to their fine artistic quality. I shall not complicate matters by discussing the type of stone used ; this was important, but not decisive, in determining style.

The widest possible variation is found in the treatment of the blocks, from the merest rubble to perfectly squared blocks regularly arranged and with a highly polished surface and knife-edge joints. The former is found in simple fortifications, not necessarily of early date, and in unimportant stretches of otherwise well-built walls, as well as in the socles of houses and other minor buildings ; the latter is found in the marble walls of temples and other important buildings, which do not directly concern us here. The Greek architects preferred to give fortification walls an appearance of rugged strength, even when using a highly artificial technique ; their sense of the fitting was perfect in this as in other things.

Dating on grounds of style is difficult, if not impossible. The old idea of a Cyclopean-polygonal-ashlar succession is unsound. Only a small proportion of the monuments can be dated at all precisely on external evidence. Walls were continually being repaired, brought up to date or extended, in more modern styles. This often complicates the problem, though sometimes it is helpful in comparative if not in absolute dating, when a series can be established on a site.

For the present I shall usually speak of sixth- to fourth-century walls in general, with occasional reference to more precise dates.

Clear-cut classification is also impossible. Styles fade into one another. The most obvious distinction in artistically finished masonry is between polygonal and squared. Polygonal again may be divided into two classes ; in the first the edges of the blocks are curved, and sometimes great undulating curves run through whole stretches of wall (see Pl. IX) ; in the other the sides are straight, producing an irregular honeycombed effect. In both there may be some approximation to courses. Scranton [9] distinguishes the former as Lesbian, after its place of origin, and the latter as true polygonal, but ‘ polygonal ’ may reasonably be used to embrace both styles. Scranton finds that Lesbian masonry is mainly archaic ; it was a dominant style in the sixth century, and is found mainly in regions of Ionian influence ; true polygonal is concentrated rather in the fifth century, though it recurs later. Polygonal work of both kinds is found mainly in terrace walls and the socles of free-standing walls. It retains most clearly the traces of its origin in rough-hewn blocks ; yet it is the most artificial of styles, involving the greatest skill and labour. Each stone required individual treatment, and lead strips were used as patterns to ensure perfect fitting. Polygonal masonry at its best has a peculiar charm, not inferior to the more austere beauty of fine ashlar.

In a style which may be considered intermediate between polygonal and ashlar, though closer to the latter, the upper and lower edges of the blocks are horizontal, but the other two often depart markedly from the vertical, producing a trapezoidal effect. This is not to be thought of as a slovenly variation on ashlar ; it is a deliberately adopted style and requires more careful fitting. Sometimes small triangular pieces, point downwards, fill interstices between the tops of the blocks. Trapezoidal work flourished particularly in the latter part of the fifth century and the first half of the fourth, when it was used in some of the very finest fortification walls. The blocks were nearly always rock-faced or very simply dressed ; this treatment suited the character of the style. In trapezoidal as also in squared work the coursing is often not regular or continuous, the height of the blocks varying considerably, apart from differences in course heights. Perfect regularity is to be looked for in the walls of temples and other enclosed buildings ; irregularities in the great fortress walls are in keeping with their general appearance of massive and rugged strength.

Squared or ashlar masonry goes back early in the history of Greek walls, and is not to be thought of as the successor of polygonal, though it superseded polygonal in the fifth century. In perfectly squared work the effects depend on the proportions of the blocks, the height of the courses and the arrangement of the blocks in them. Proportions vary widely ; but Attic masons seem to have found their ideal in the constantly recurring ratio of 1 unit of height to about 2·6 of length, which in many examples amounts to $1\frac{1}{2}$ by 4 Attic feet. But different walls were built on different principles ; proportions together with edging emphasize sometimes the individual blocks, sometimes the courses, sometimes — especially in fine marble walls — the indivisibility of the whole. Course heights are sometimes equal (' isodomic '), sometimes alternately high and low, sometimes varied (often decreasing upwards). Headers and stretchers are used in a variety of schemes or in no particular scheme. Increasingly in careful work the vertical joints were kept in line throughout the height of the wall.

Last but far from least important in defining the character of a wall is the treatment of the surface of the blocks. It ranges from ' rock-faced ' or ' quarry-faced ' work (sometimes called ' rusticated '), in which the face of the block forms a rough convex, more or less as the stone left the quarry, to a surface which is carefully flattened and smoothed. The rock face is naturally left in stonework which is of little importance or which would seldom or never be seen (*e.g.* because buried) ; but it is also deliberately retained in some buildings as more suitable than an artificial finish ; or else it is slightly modified by rough grooves or striations. There are also a number of more decorative schemes, mostly consisting of rows of short vertical grooves. The treatment is sometimes varied in different parts of a wall ; for example, a wall of more careful finish may be placed on a rock-faced socle, which makes a subtle transition from the native rock. In fine masonry *anathyrosis* was used, *i.e.* the exceptionally careful fitting of a narrow strip along the edges ; and the joints were sometimes elaborated by various forms of drafting (the chiselling of a flat strip along the margins of the outer face) and bevelling ; the angles of towers are often emphasized by drafting.

Amongst the various styles and techniques one thinks of quarry-faced or simply dressed limestone masonry, ashlar or trapezoidal, or more probably both, as typical of the noblest city and fortress walls of Greece. The men who built these walls were fine masons and engineers and architects, and artists of a high order. Their work shows how foreign to Greek ideas is our distinction between ' workman ', ' craftsman ' and ' artist ' ; *techne* embraces all these. The Greek artist's love of beauty and unerring sense of fitness and proportion and endless capacity for taking pains, seen at their best in the Parthenon or a Polycleitan athlete, came into play in the shaping of a simple block and the building of a wall.

IV

THE AGORA[1]

ACCORDING to Herodotus (i. 153) Cyrus king of
Persia said of the Greeks, ' I never yet feared the
kind of men who have a place set apart in the
middle of the city in which they get together and tell
one another lies under oath '. Like other despots, he had
a misplaced contempt for freer institutions ; but at least
he had sufficient insight into Greek life to regard the agora
as particularly characteristic of the people. The word
' agora ' is quite untranslatable, since it stands for something as peculiarly Hellenic as polis, or *sophrosyne*. One
may doubt whether the public places of any other cities
have ever seen such an intense and sustained concentration
of varied activities. The agora was in fact no mere public
place but the central zone of the city, its living heart.
In spite of an inevitable diffusion and specialization of
functions, it retained a real share of all its old miscellaneous
functions. It remained essentially a single whole, or at
least strongly resisted division. It was the constant resort
of all citizens, and it did not spring to life on special
occasions but was the daily scene of social life, business
and politics.

Like the city as a whole, it began in a simple way. A
fairly level open space was all that was needed. A good
water supply was important, and satisfactory drainage.
A roughly central site was adopted if possible, since the
agora had to provide a convenient focus for city life in

general and for the main streets which meandered through the residential quarters and radiated onwards through the country outside. The early dominance of the acropolis naturally affected the position of the agora, but in time, as we have seen, the emphasis was reversed, and the acropolis was now an appendage of the city, the agora its true centre which held the whole structure together.

In form the early agora was no doubt extremely simple. The same free space sufficed for all kinds of purposes. Here the people could assemble to be harangued ; the only equipment needed was some sort of tribune for the speakers, and possibly seats for men of dignity. Religious assemblies at the festivals could use the same place, and it was convenient if the agora, or part of it, had a roughly ' theatral ' shape, that is, if there was a convenient slope which could be provided with tiers of steps for the audience. The ' theatral areas ' of Minoan towns may possibly be the forerunners of such an arrangement ; the agora of Lato had broad steps rising on its northern side ; the little ' theatres ' of certain Attic demes may be simple local agoras ; and the steps cut in the hillside on the west of the Athenian agora, though attributed by H. A. Thompson to the fifth century, and by R. Martin to early archaic times,[2] are agreed by both to have been intended for spectators at shows. The classical Greek theatre may be considered a sort of duplicate agora, detached from the old centre and highly developed in a certain way for special purposes. A very simple ' change of scene ' was needed to turn the primitive agora, or a part of it, into a market ; temporary booths could be set up for the purpose.

It was difficult for the agora, embedded in the middle,

to expand with the growth of the city. Still, on fortunate sites it was possible. At Athens there is somewhat shadowy literary evidence for a primitive agora west of the Acropolis,[3] and the classical agora may be the result of a northward shift of the centre of gravity in the seventh and sixth centuries. In another way, too, the strain on the agora could be eased as population grew and the place became more and more built up and bestrewn with monuments. The bigger political and religious gatherings found roomier accommodation elsewhere, especially in the theatre, which was often used for the general assembly as well as for plays. The Athenians constructed a special place for their Ecclesia, the Pnyx, on a hillside to the south-west, though they still occasionally assembled in the agora, for example when they wished to ostracize inconvenient politicians.

Architecturally the growth of the agora meant more and better buildings. The council-house, the prytaneion, offices for individual magistrates and boards, record offices and so forth were naturally placed in, or at least very near the agora, unless some local tradition kept them rooted on the acropolis or placed them elsewhere. The stoa or open colonnade, with or without appendages, was found to be a useful general-purpose building and became especially characteristic of the agora. As the cults of the city multiplied and grew the agora received a large share of altars and temples, and rivalled or surpassed the acropolis in the number and variety of its cults, if not in venerability. The increasing complexity of business life was reflected most clearly in the agora. Archaic Greece saw a tremendous growth in trade and industry and the leading commercial cities gained an important place in Mediterranean markets. Wine, oil, pottery and other manufactures were exported ; essential foodstuffs such as corn had to be imported. Wholesale merchants, speculators and bankers arose ; these had their establishments near the agora or the harbour (which often meant the same thing), but also used the stoas, whose adaptability enabled them to be used as exchanges and market-halls. The old market continued, with its booths, but from the fifth century dignified halls were increasingly built, still in the form of stoas, or rows of shops were given a fine columnar façade.

The stoas and temples dominated the agora. To complete the picture one has to imagine a variety of minor monuments, grouped like the larger buildings, irregularly but not necessarily inartistically. A fountain-house — not a merely decorative fountain — was often an important element. Statues of gods, heroes and men were set up in front of the buildings and along the streets which led into and through the area. Trees were planted to provide shade in addition to that of the stoas. Paving was confined to limited areas until late.

The growth was slow, piecemeal and irregular, and its result was not a clearly marked architectural type. The agoras of the old towns vary greatly in form, arrangement and contents. A certain degree of architectural unity might be imposed, varying with local factors, but close coordination was not to be expected, still less formal symmetry.

Again, archaic material is scanty and difficult to disentangle. The small agora of Lato in Crete, already mentioned, was built on a terrace and formed a rough pentagon. Streets entered it from various directions ;

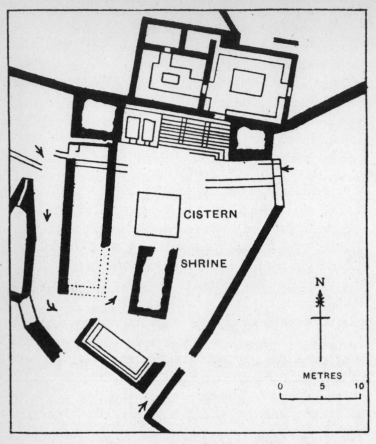

FIG. 10.   Lato, agora (after *B.C.H.* xvii, Pls. IV-V)

there was a stoa on the west and another on the south, and a sacred enclosure and a cistern in the middle. Most interesting was the north side. The steps mentioned above clearly formed an auditorium from which spectacles could be seen or speakers heard in the open space below. They were flanked by towers standing in the line of an inner fortification, and at the top was a building which may be identified as the Prytancion. Thus in position and form the place has many features typical of the early agora.[4] A curiously similar early agora has been found at Dreros, also in Crete ; it too is just below a saddle connecting two hills, one of which was the acropolis, and it contains a set of ' theatral ' steps, an interesting archaic temple, and a complex of rooms which may have been the Prytaneion.

Athens now provides our best object-lesson, which is as we would wish. The American excavations of the nineteen-thirties almost completed the tremendous task of clearing the agora district, in the heart of modern as of ancient Athens, and though the results were not spectacular, and though many problems of topography are still unsolved, a fairly clear and trustworthy outline of the architectural development can be given.[5] The site of the classical agora is admirable for the purpose. It is north-west of the Acropolis, from which it is easily and quickly accessible. From a fairly extensive and level central space the ground rises very gently on the east and more steeply on the west, while to the south is the rocky Areopagus, below which rise copious springs, and on the north, providing adequate drainage, is the Eridanus stream.

The agora seems to have begun to grow on this site at the end of the seventh century, spreading outwards from the point on the west side where the Council-House stood. We learn something of earlier uses to which the ground was put from a long series of graves and from the traditional name of the whole district, Kerameikos, or potters' quarter. Very ancient streets traversed the area, one diagonally from N.W. to S.E. and on to the Acropolis, another from north to south along the western side ; and

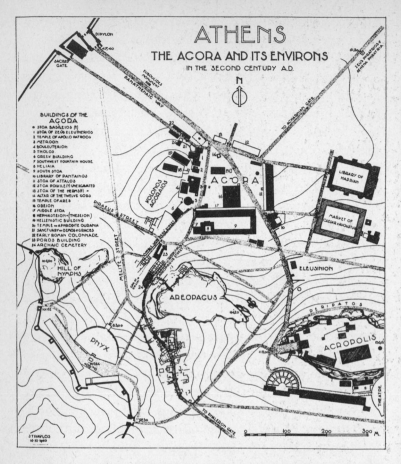

FIG. 11. Athens, agora and surrounding district (by J. Travlos)

these continued to be used and the second especially had a decisive effect on the ultimate plan of the agora.

The earliest remains are on the site of the Council-House, towards the southern end of the west side ; [6] they may go back as early as the seventh century, but most of the monuments of the archaic agora belong to the sixth. Cults of civic importance were established near by. Just north of the Council-House a small apsidal temple was built for Apollo, and beyond it Zeus had a simple shrine. So the embryo civic and religious centre was taking shape. South of the Council-House a curious building, irregularly planned round a court with colonnades, was probably the forerunner of the Tholos on whose future site it stood, serving as a kind of duplicate Prytaneion. The tyrants of Athens, Peisistratus and his sons, made their contribution. Thucydides tells (ii. 15) how they constructed the chief fountain-house of Athens, Enneakrounos. Where this was is a notorious problem of Athenian topography ; the excavators have found a fountain-house on the south side of the agora, and call it Enneakrounos, but the identification is not yet established.[7] The great drain which runs from south to north under the street on the west side, and which the excavators were able to put into service again to prevent flooding, is assigned to the time of the tyrants. That the agora was now taking definite shape is indicated by several sixth-century boundary stones (with inscriptions, 'I am the boundary of the agora' and the like) which have turned up. Late in the century an altar of the twelve gods was dedicated, which was to serve as a central milestone of the Attic road system, showing that the spot was thought of as the centre not only of Athens but of all Attica ; towards the north end the Americans have found a small square enclosure associated with this shrine. Finally, perhaps in the time of Cleisthenes the democratic reformer, a worthier Council-House was built, and a little to the north a small temple of the Mother of the Gods, with whose cult the Council-House and the

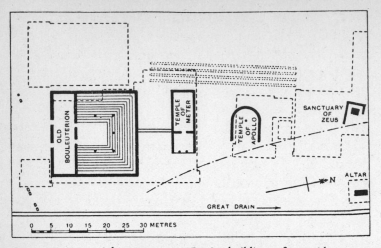

Fig. 12. Athens, agora, pre-Persian buildings of west side
(*Hesperia*, vi, p. 133, fig. 72)
Dotted lines show position of later buildings

city archives were long closely associated. Athens now had a modest but dignified civic centre; it was given a certain unity by the fact that the chief monuments were placed in line along a straight north-to-south street. We may infer from later indications that the market was concentrated mainly on the east side, where the great market-hall of Attalus ultimately stood.

Like the Acropolis and the rest of Athens, the agora suffered badly in the Persian wars, and the temples and public buildings were reduced more or less to ruins. Recovery was slow and piecemeal. Indeed, part of the site at least seems to have become a real Kerameikos again — remains of potters' workshops, and of metal-workers' too, have been found in the north-west where the stoa of Zeus later stood. The new buildings were bigger and architecturally finer, but they were still treated as self-contained units and most of them were strung out along the western side again. First came the Tholos, a small but elegant round building towards the southern end, which was a sort of annexe of the Prytaneion and was used by the standing committee of Council. The old Bouleuterion was perhaps patched up and did duty for a time. The Metroön (shrine of the Mother) was not yet rebuilt, nor did Apollo get his temple back till the fourth century. Cimon took an interest in the agora, and planted plane trees in it and laid the bones of the hero Theseus, recovered from Scyros, in a shrine, the site of which is not known ; [8] and it was a member of his family, one Peisianax, who had a stoa built which was destined to become very famous as the Poikile or Painted Stoa ; it probably stood on the north side and its remains have not been found. The fine Doric temple which still stands almost complete on the hill to the west was built soon after the middle of the fifth century. Though not in the agora proper, it must have dominated this side and improved its appearance while it was still in an unsatisfactory state. The claims of various deities to this temple, which was long known as the ' Theseum ', have been energetically championed by archaeologists. Hephaestus has now been fairly securely installed, though there is still some jostling ; the discovery of traces of bronzefounding near by confirm the claim of the god of metal workers. The agora must have been constantly finding room for less conspicuous cults which have not left considerable remains.[9] A little later than the Hephaestus temple another large Doric temple was built, in the middle of the agora ; at least that is where its foundations have come to light, but Dinsmoor has shown[10] that it

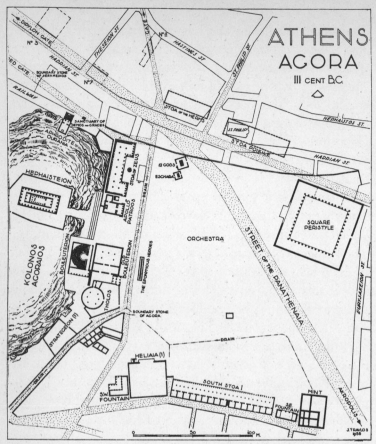

FIG. 13. Athens, agora, third century B.C. (by J. Travlos)

The South Stoa was built late in the fifth century B.C.; the rooms behind it were either shops or magistrates' offices.

The square enclosure adjoining it on the west is thought to have been a law court; it was archaic in its original form though several times remodelled (see fig. 24).

The colonnaded enclosure, dated in the fourth century (it was never finished) replaced a simpler late fifth century building probably identified by the finds as a law-court.

The mint, to the south-east, is identified by the evidence of coin-striking found in it.

The 'orchestra' probably marks the site of the primitive theatre.

For the fountain-houses see fig. 24 and Ch. VIII, supplementary note.

was originally built to the east of the agora and moved to its final site only in Augustan times. In any case the central area of the agora was kept largely free from major monuments until late. A few years later a fine Doric stoa with projecting gabled wings was built at the north end of the west side (see p. 113) ; this building, says H. A. Thompson,[11] ' follows closely in the full tradition of Periclean architecture ', and is not unworthy of the architect of the Propylaea. It was sacred to Zeus God of Freedom, and was probably also the Royal Stoa, no less famous than the Poikile. Finally, towards the end of the century, a new Council-House was built (see p. 129), well designed but unobtrusively placed behind the old one, which may have continued in use as a record office. The classical agora was now complete ; [12] only small additions were made during the next two centuries — and of course the statues and minor monuments were multiplying all the time — until there came a spectacular outburst of renewed building under the patronage of Hellenistic monarchs.

As a sustained effort of reconstruction after the devastation of war, the fifth-century agora of Athens will furnish an interesting comparison with Miletus, and is not without interest today. As individual buildings the two principal stoas are worthy to rank with the masterpieces of the Acropolis, but there was only a limited degree of coordination in the general plan, which in principle was similar to its archaic forerunner. The new agora of Athens was old-fashioned in type. It is difficult to imagine the general effect, but one suspects it was a little scrappy, though not necessarily unpleasing. The buildings mentioned belonged mostly to the ' civic centre ', though the stoas were sometimes used for business. The market seems to have covered an ill-defined area on the east, north and west (especially perhaps the east) with a tendency to encroach on the political agora. To a limited extent different spheres of activity were separated but the agora was still essentially *one*.

The centre of Corinth too has been fully excavated, but the site was greatly complicated by rebuilding in Roman times, and in spite of very interesting early monuments gives a much less clear picture of the classical agora. A fine position with access to two seas and a magnificent acropolis marked out Corinth as a place of great commercial as well as strategic possibilities. The town spread out to the north of the Acrocorinthus, and in the middle was the low hill on which the columns of the archaic temple of Apollo still stand, dominating the site. South-east of the hill was the fountain of Peirene, which ' served at all times as the focus of Corinthian civic activity '.[13] From early archaic times the shallow depression north of Peirene and east of the temple hill was an important centre. A series of fifth-century colonnaded shops has been found facing this area from the west. On the north side of the hill, too, a number of stoas succeeded one another at various dates. Towards the end of the fifth century a large area south of the hill was cleared, and in time this became the main agora ; later a stoa was built along the northern edge, south of the temple, and the southern limit was defined by a very long stoa with a double row of shops and store-rooms behind. There were a number of small shrines in the area and several roads converged here.

Elis deserves special mention because of Pausanias' com-

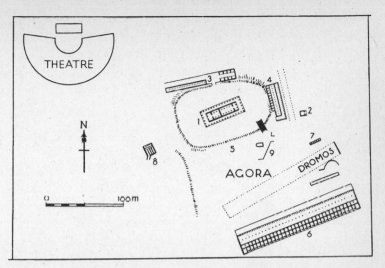

FIG. 14. Corinth, agora district, c. 300 B.C. (provisional, after J. Travlos, by courtesy of the American School of Classical Studies at Athens)

1. Temple of Apollo
2. Temple
3. N. stoa and bath-house (gymnasium ?)
4. 'N. Building' (shops and colonnade)
5. Site of later N.W. stoa
6. South Stoa
7. Fountain of Peirene
8. Fountain of Glauke
9. Fountain, with triglyph wall

Dotted line shows race-course, with starting line at E. end (p. 156)

ment on it and because it has been carefully studied by F. Tritsch as a specimen of the old-fashioned type of agora (old fashioned but not actually *old*; Elis was founded in 471 B.C. and the agora took shape in the course of the fifth century). Pausanias says (vi. 24. 2): ' The agora of Elis is not after the fashion of the cities of Ionia . . .' (what this means we shall soon see); ' it is built in the older manner, with stoas standing independently of one another and with streets between them'. The picture he gives is of an area cut up by streets and with stoas placed as separate units about it. The most important buildings discovered are in fact two very long stoas,

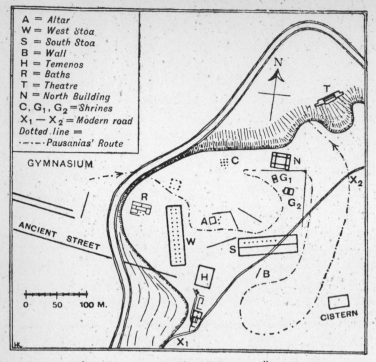

A = Altar
W = West Stoa
S = South Stoa
B = Wall
H = Temenos
R = Baths
T = Theatre
N = North Building
C, G₁, G₂ = Shrines
X₁ — X₂ = Modern road
Dotted line =
·—·—· Pausanias' Route

GYMNASIUM

ANCIENT STREET

0   50   100 M.

FIG. 15. Elis, excavations in and around agora (Ö. J., xxvii, p. 68, fig. 77)

built probably towards the end of the fifth century; they are roughly at right angles, but they are different in form and widely separated and are far from forming regular sides of a square. Shrines, altars and minor monuments have been found too, and the offices, temples and hero-tombs mentioned by Pausanias complete the picture.

There was no more uniformity about the old-fashioned agoras than about the towns to which they belonged. For instance at Thera, where the ancient city was built on a long ridge, the agora was little more than a pronounced widening of a main street which ran along the ridge, at its highest point just under the summit.[14]

The archaeological remains are the dry and dusty bones of the agora ; to clothe them with flesh and blood one must say a little more about its varied life, of which literature tells us a great deal, especially at Athens. The part played by the agora in politics should be clear by now, and something more will be said of it in dealing with the Council-House and other elements. Magistrates multiplied in a great city like Athens, and most of them had quarters in the agora ; a whole area in the southwest was called ' the offices '.[15] Politics was closely bound up with the law-courts. The Athenian legal system was very remarkable ; strange ancient courts sat in strange places (Pausanias i. 28. 6–11). But the great democratic court, the Heliaea, had its seat in the agora ; and we read in Demosthenes (xxv. 23) how the Areopagus sat in the Royal Stoa, roped off to keep unruly crowds away. From the beginning the agora had been associated with the administration of justice ; already in Homer we see a case being tried in the presence of the people ' in the agora ' (*Iliad* xviii. 497 ff. ; cf. *Iliad* xi. 807 and *Odyssey* xii. 439), though it must be remembered that by ' agora ' Homer often means simply ' assembly '.

No clear line was drawn between civic centre and market. The public buildings and shrines were in the agora ; meat and fish and the rest were sold in the same agora ; and *agorazein* means to go to market, to buy, though also occasionally to stroll about the agora. At Athens quarters were devoted to the sale (sometimes also the manufacture) of particular wares, and called after these (the fish, the vegetables — including the onions, the garlic and so on — the bronzes, the slaves, and many others).

Booksellers, we may infer from Plato's *Apology* (26 D), had their stalls by the old orchestra. On a higher financial plane, the bankers too had a quarter ; they were still called ' men-with-tables ' like simple money-changers, but by Demosthenes' time they were business magnates with large staffs.

Marketing ' when the agora was full ', *i.e.* in the morning, must have been a noisy and nerve-racking business, with much haggling. The fishmongers had a particularly bad reputation ; according to the comic poets they used the Greek equivalent of ' Billingsgate ', glared at their customers like Gorgons, asked exorbitant prices with a take-it-or-leave-it air, and faked rotten fish. Most cities had officials called *agoranomoi* to exercise control and ensure fair dealing. Athens had, in addition, corn-inspectors for a particularly vital trade and inspectors of weights and measures. We read in inscriptions of the agoranomoi seeing that agora and streets are kept clean and tidy and watching relations between employers and employed.

This busy commercial life concentrated in the agora was a vital element in the prosperity of democratic Athens. But for some people of a conservative and somewhat snobbish turn of mind it seemed petty and degrading and vulgar. For these same people the agora was the haunt of the dregs of the populace, the home of idleness, vulgarity and gossip. Look at the agora for a moment through Aristophanes' eyes. In the *Knights*, Demosthenes tells the Sausage-Seller, ' You are a cheeky rascal from the agora ' (181 ; cf. 293, 636, 1258). In the *Clouds*, when the Just Logos and the Unjust are urging the benefits of their different systems of education, the

Just says (991, 1003), 'You will learn to hate the agora
. . . you will spend your time bright and shining in
the gymnasia not chattering in the agora'. The agora
was the chief place to which men would drift in moments
of leisure to find congenial company, in the stoas, under
the plane trees, in the barbers' shops or the wine-shops or
by the smiths' fires.[16] The result might well be waste of
time, malicious gossip and worse. It was no doubt dis-
approval of the vulgarity of the agora which made
Aristotle recommend (*Politics* vii. 11. 2) that as in Thessaly
there should be one agora free from trade and of a religious (and, it appears, somewhat snobbish) character and
another for buying and selling ; note that Aristotle says
that it ought to be so, not that it is so, and goes to Thessaly
for an example ; in fact the Greeks thoroughly mixed
up the elements of their lives, for better or for worse,
and this fusion is clearly seen in the agora.

Aristophanes is being very unfair in seeing nothing
but evil in the more informal life of the agora. Some
of the ' idlers ' idled to good purpose. Socrates was
one of them. In the *Apology* (17 C) he warns the jury
that they must not expect fine rhetoric from him, but
the style which they have often heard him using in the
agora. 'You are always babbling about cobblers and
fullers and such paltry folk ', says Callicles in the *Gorgias*
(491 A), impatient of Socrates' homely illustrations ; it
was in their quarters in the agora that Socrates found
them. Socrates was unique, but for many others too,
when they got together in the stoas, the talk must have
turned to ethical or metaphysical subjects, and the discussions would be spontaneous, frank and spirited. A
particular speaker might have a favourite spot and a

favourite time and a regular group of associates, and thus the first step was taken towards the creation of a philosophical school ; but when regular schools grew at Athens in the fourth century most of them required more secluded quarters and found them in the suburban gymnasia. But the free and lively spirit of the agora made a vital contribution to Greek philosophy.

A religious element pervaded the agora ; the public buildings were dedicated to deities and there were altars and shrines everywhere. ' The agora ', says Fougères, writing of Mantinea,[17] ' is a sort of holy place, a *temenos* inhabited by the protecting deities, haunted by legendary ancestors and the shades of great citizens. . . . Around the common hearth one breathes the atmosphere of the distant past, of common glory, of patriotic piety.' This goes a little too far ; recall the same Fougères writing of the acropolis (p. 37 above). At Athens it must have been difficult to get away from the atmosphere of the immediate present ; no part of the agora had a cloistral air. The cults show an endless variety, besides those most obviously connected with public life. Hermes, as the patron of traders, was in a special sense the god of the market. Hero-shrines, often with the grave of the hero or a legendary founder, were frequent.

The part played by the agora in festivals and games, and its connection with the theatre, have already been mentioned. Many interesting traditions preserved something of the connection. At Sparta a part of the agora was called Choros, and in it the young men danced in honour of Apollo at the festival called Gymnopaedia ; at Elis the agora was called Hippodrome (Pausanias iii. 11. 9, vi. 24. 2).

Finally, both religion and political life were closely bound up with art, and again you find an intense concentration in the agora. Nowhere, except in the famous national shrines like Olympia, would one see such an impressive conglomeration of temples, stoas and other fine buildings as in the agora of a great and ancient city ; or such an array of sculpture in and around them ; and many small towns had their share of masterpieces too. The great paintings in the stoas deserve special mention ; they have now been completely lost, but in their day they ranked with the finest sculpture.

We have still to see the place taken by the agora in Hippodamian cities. Hardly anything is known of the ' Hippodameia ' at Peiraeus. Apparently it was still fairly open in the fourth century, since we hear [18] of a house standing on it. Pausanias says (i. 1. 3) that Peiraeus had one agora near the sea and another inland — an unusual arrangement, but we must remember that Peiraeus was not a true *city* but the harbour town of Athens. In mercantile cities by the sea, the agora, though often closely associated with the harbour, was not a mere extension of the quaysides, but something greater and more or less distinct. At Miletus, we shall see, the agora area tended to resolve itself into a north part by the harbour and a south part somewhat detached, but it still remained essentially *one*.

Miletus will best repay study. Architectural growth hardly began before the fourth century. Among the earliest important buildings was a large house-like structure, occupying two house-blocks (a common unit at Miletus), which was probably a prytaneion and was later incorporated in the north agora complex. A long stoa,

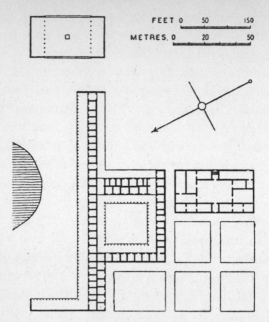

Fig. 16. Miletus, north agora, end of fourth century B.C. (after *Milet*,
i. 6, Taf. xxiii)

like those which bordered the harbour at Peiraeus, was
built facing north towards the harbour, with small rooms
behind it ; a short wing made a return northwards at
the western end, and opposite this on the east was the enclosure of the shrine of Apollo Delphinios. Attached to
the stoa in the rear was a square colonnaded court. The
harbour building was the first important architectural
scheme of the new agora, and besides giving the town
a fine water-front, provided facilities for the merchants
as Miletus' mercantile prosperity returned. The harbour
zone was, naturally, developed first.

The distinguishing feature of Ionian agora-planning is
beginning to appear in this complex. The architects who

adorned the older cities' agoras created several forms of
stoa which as units were both practically and artistically
satisfying. The Ionian architects realized and explored the
possibilities of combining stoas at right angles, fitting
them into the rectangular street system, and so forming
effective and impressive schemes. There were various
possibilities, as one can see especially well at Miletus,
and one need not single out a particular combination as
the regular type. Before good examples were revealed
by excavation it was often assumed that the ideal consisted
of four stoas completely enclosing a rectangular space.
This idea dies hard, though thoroughly disproved.[19]
Vitruvius certainly says (v. 1) that the Greeks built their
' fora ' ' in quadrato '; but he is describing a late type.
We shall see presently the limited part played by the
peristyle ' agora '. An arrangement which was repeatedly
found convenient was the so-called ' horseshoe ',[20] in
which three stoas formed three sides of a rectangle, the
fourth generally being occupied by an important street
with various public buildings or another stoa beyond it.

To return to Miletus — the ' horseshoe ' was introduced in a modified form and on a vast scale in the south
agora-complex, on which building activity was concentrated in the course of the third century, though possibly
it was planned earlier. On the east a long stoa was built
with a single colonnade and with three rows of rooms
behind, serving no doubt as shops and storehouses. Facing
it on the west were two L-shaped stoas with double
colonnades, of which only the southern had rooms behind.
The west side was thus not a continuous stoa as was the
corresponding south side at Priene, and additional means
of access to the vast place was provided; but the unity

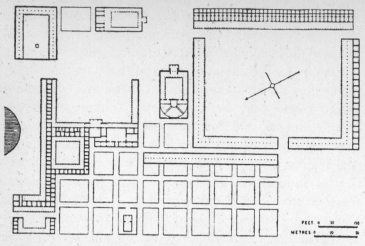

FIG. 17. Miletus, agora, middle of second century B.C. (after *Milet*, i. 2, Abb. 53; i. 6, Taf. xxiv and i. 7, Abb. 40)

and grandeur of the whole design was hardly impaired by this, or by the fact that the process of building required so long and probably fell into several stages — the south wing, which appears to have been two-storeyed, may be as late as the middle of the second century B.C. The architects who succeeded one another in carrying out the great work maintained its unity and also its subordination to the general street-plan of Miletus.

The south agora, says von Gerkan (p. 100), was conceived as ' Staatsmarkt ' ; but the east stoa, an important and probably early part of the scheme, was, as he affirms, devoted to trade. The huge scale of the stoas, their openness and freedom in large sections from encumbering rooms, may have given to the south agora more civic dignity than the north possessed ; but the two areas are not to be differentiated clearly or opposed to one another in function. The political centre of Miletus was perhaps defined as being between them, by the erection of the Council-House, a covered theatre with a colonnaded court in front, between 175 and 164 B.C.

The north complex had undergone little extension for some time, except that a small ' horseshoe ' had been placed behind the west wing ; but in the middle of the second century, with the addition of an L-shaped wing on the south-east, another and much larger ' horseshoe ' was formed. What is probably a small temple was unobtrusively inserted in the long west side ; the colonnades incidentally provided it with a fine forecourt. In this arrangement we see a certain tendency towards strictly axial planning, but it is not very pronounced ; emphatic symmetry about a well-marked axis is not characteristic of the Ionian agora. The east side, opposite the temple, was left quite open for a while, though some distance further east, south of the colonnaded court of the Delphinion, a rectangular gymnasium was erected.

At this stage — towards the close of the Hellenistic period and before the period of Roman domination — the Milesian agora had attained a well-developed and satisfying form, which the renewed building of the Roman imperial age, following a period of depression in Asia under the Roman republic, could elaborate and complicate according to the fashions of the time without making any real improvement. To reach this stage we have had to pursue the process of growth well down into Hellenistic times ; yet no important element has appeared which can be called specifically Hellenistic or unclassical. The architects were guided throughout by the original rectangular street-plan of the city, and made good use of the opportunities it left them ; the result was worthy of a great city. The Council-House marked the political centre, with the maritime agora on one side, and the great south agora, for business not immediately connected with the sea and for recreation and general purposes, on the other. The design was simple and spacious, aesthetically pleasing and practically convenient.

Priene is much simpler, but equally characteristic in its smaller way. The agora was planned with the rest of the city in the fourth century. Two complete house-blocks or insulae were kept open ; along the north ran an important east-to-west street, and to increase the open space the stoas which ran along the east, south and west forming a ' horseshoe ' were placed outside the edge of the two insulae, pushing the streets considerably outwards — an unusual arrangement — though the original line of the south street was continued by steps leading up into

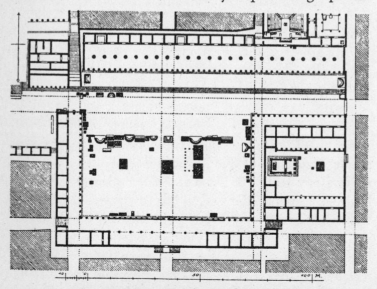

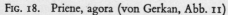

FIG. 18. Priene, agora (von Gerkan, Abb. 11)

the south colonnade. Behind the three stoas were shops, but in the middle of the south side these were omitted and the colonnade doubled to form a large hall. The temple of Athena looked down on the agora from the north-west, and the temple of Zeus was placed back to back with the east stoa, in a little court of its own. As usual, the stoas of the main square were not allowed to degenerate into a mere setting for a temple ; they stood entirely in their own right. An altar stood in the centre of the agora, and other smaller monuments accumulated along the north street and in front of the stoas ; but the area embraced by the stoas was kept free from larger structures.

A small area behind the western colonnade was intended for the fish- and meat-market — stone tables have been found in place. Again we find a tendency to segregate trade at least in its less dignified forms, but even on these carefully planned sites it was not carried very far. The agora was still not clearly divisible according to function ; even less were there two agoras, one political, one commercial. Closely related stoas still served a variety of purposes. Their rooms are often difficult to identify ; many were shops, some government offices, some shrines. At Priene the civic buildings were mostly on the north side, but still formed part of the agora group. On this side in the second century the magnificent north stoa was built, replacing a more modest predecessor and forming a façade, at its eastern end, for the Assembly-Room and the Prytaneion. The stoa was called Sacred and contained shrines, public records and offices. Altogether the city centre of Priene was architecturally fine and admirably adapted to the citizens' needs ;

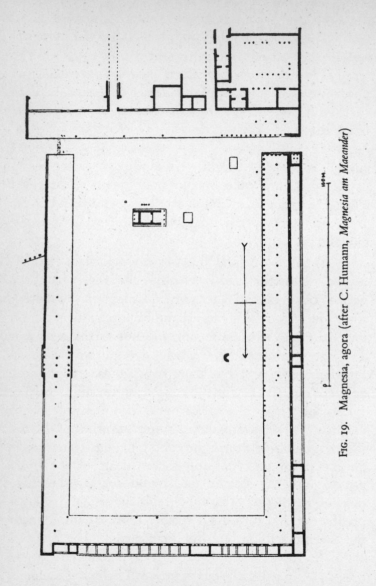

FIG. 19. Magnesia, agora (after C. Humann, *Magnesia am Maeander*)

and it blended perfectly into the design of the town, giving an organic structure to the gridiron plan, which is apt to become formless and monotonous.

Another Ionian town, Magnesia on the Maeander, will provide a third example. In the fourth century the city was transferred to a new site, and the agora took shape in the following century. It occupied six insulae in a rectangular street scheme. The new temple of the ancient shrine of Artemis, and its colonnaded court, retained a distinctly different orientation, and where shrine and agora came into contact the latter had the best of it and the sacred enclosure was cut off obliquely. A little temple of Zeus stood upon the open area of the agora ; but it was small and not centrally placed, and was in fact hardly more than the most important of the minor monuments. Again the great double stoas dominate the plan. This agora was second only to the south market of Miletus in size. It was not quite rectangular — its long sides converged slightly towards the south. Two long sides and one short formed a ' horseshoe,' instead of the more usual two short and one long ; this arrangement shows a tendency towards more complete enclosure which became increasingly marked. Behind the north and west stoas were a number of rooms, most of which were shops, though two were shrines and one a fountain-house ; behind the western part of the detached stoa on the south was what appears to be a prytaneion. The variety of function of the buildings connected with the agora may again be noted.

Miletus and Priene, and to a lesser degree Magnesia, may at this stage of their history be taken as examples of the true ' Ionian ' agora, the type evolved to suit Hippodamian town-planning. This type was still a classical Greek agora in the full sense. Comparison with the old-fashioned agora shows an obvious difference in form, arising out of the new method of placing the stoas and the imposition of a rigid order, but also a similarity in spirit. The true Hellenic agora was the inner zone, the nucleus, and was closely knit into the fabric of the city. Public activities were concentrated and mingled in it. The Greek did not sort out his life into neat insulated compartments, but let each element act upon the others, and the agora is a manifestation of this spirit. All this is true of the Ionian agora with only a little modification; the activities of the citizens merged there, and varied streams of energy flowed freely in. The agora was still directly involved in the street system,[21] and was not exclusive or segregated from the rest, but vitally linked with it. Thus one may call the Ionian agora a classical Hellenic creation, though only brought to completion in the Hellenistic age ; it was a continuation of the work of Hippodamus ; it shows dignity, restraint and orderliness of design, and although the fifth-century exquisiteness of form has gone, deserves to be given a place among the notable achievements of Hellenic architecture.

The Ionian type was by no means universally adopted, even in Asia Minor. Less regular agoras were still built and at the same time new and more thoroughly Hellenistic ideas were put into practice. The agora of Assos was irregular, but its north and south sides consisted of long stoas of typically Pergamene form (see p. 115). Pergamon itself possessed two so-called agoras. The lower was a slightly irregular quadrilateral, completely enclosed by two-storeyed colonnades, a fine market-

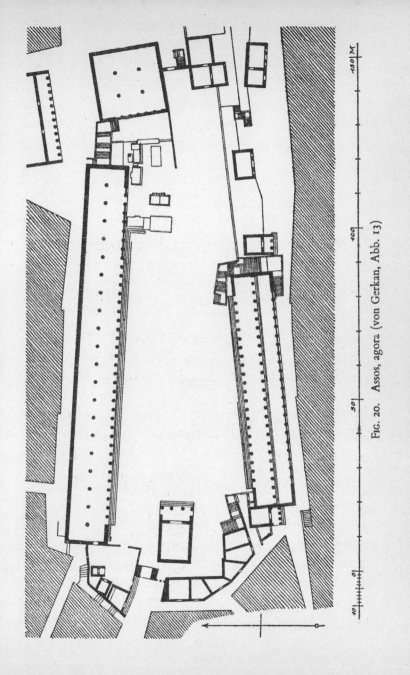

FIG. 20. Assos, agora (von Gerkan, Abb. 13)

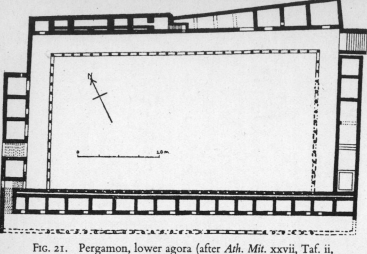

FIG. 21. Pergamon, lower agora (after *Ath. Mit.* xxvii, Taf. ii,
and xxix, Taf. vii)

building, but not an agora in the full sense ; ' it was not
an element in the town-plan ', says von Gerkan (p. 102),
' but an independent building, separated from its surroundings '. The ' upper agora ' (fig. 7) was the tail-end
of the ambitious architectural design carried out on the
acropolis ; the terrace of the great altar of Zeus cut into
it ; it reproduces, in a highly sophisticated form, the old
dependence of agora on acropolis.

Hellenistic Delos too will offer an interesting contrast
and several incidental points of interest. In this age the
sacred island of Apollo became a great international
market, and its architectural growth was spectacular.
Various monarchs and trading corporations contributed
and the result showed a certain lack of balance and unity.
The agora proper was concentrated south of the sanctuary of Apollo and east of the harbour ; here in the

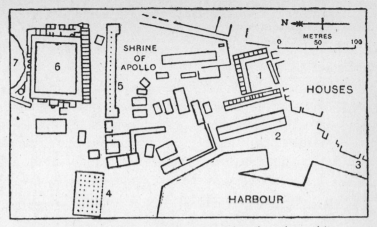

FIG. 22. Delos, central area (after P. Roussel, *Délos, colonie athénienne,*
plan at end)

1. Agora   4. Hypostyle Hall
2. Stoa of Philip   5. Stoa of Antigonus
3. Warehouses   6. Agora of Italians
            7. Sacred Lake

third and second centuries were built a number of stoas
which formed a loosely coordinated scheme.[22]   Large
warehouses lined the quays stretching southwards (fig.
22.3), and to the north too were imposing buildings of
commercial and social importance. The remarkable
Hypostyle (columnar) Hall was a sort of Exchange. The
biggest single building in Delos was the so-called ' agora
of the Italians ',[23] built at the end of the second century
by and for the most numerous corporation of merchants,
as a *lieu de réunion*. It was a great quadrilateral court
completely enclosed by Doric colonnades with rooms
and exedras behind. This exclusive and self-contained
form was appropriate since it was not a public agora but
a private club ; but the conception was alien to true
Greek agora-planning. Altogether the central area of

Delos formed a cosmopolitan Hellenistic trading centre, hemming in the temples and stoas of the ancient shrine of Apollo. It had the irregularity of the old agora with perhaps even less unity.[24]

The form of the Italian building raises the question of the part played by the enclosed peristyle court in agora-planning. The idea that the peristyle was the ideal form of agora, the culmination of a process in which the Priene type was an intermediate stage, seems plausible at first sight. But if our view of the real nature of the agora is correct, the peristyle was different in conception from both the classical types; in its complete enclosure and seclusion from the city around it contained an alien element which made it less fully an agora. The ideal was approached, if anywhere, at Miletus and Priene.

In the fourth century and Hellenistic age the peristyle court played an increasingly important part in architecture.[25] It was used in houses, gymnasia and the forecourts of sacred and civic buildings. It could serve as a market-building, as an element in the agora; we have already met examples, to which may be added an example at Athens, a peristyle 59 m. square, of the fourth century or late fifth, of which the remains have been found under the stoa of Attalus (see fig. 13). In late Hellenistic and Roman times there was a greater tendency to plan the main agora-square as a whole on this principle, to make it an enclosed building turning in upon itself. City life had lost something of its old quality, and the agora had a less vital part to play, a less intimate relation with all the varied activities of the community. In some cases the influence of the Roman forum is clearly at work; the forum, though it takes on a variety of forms, shows a general tendency to

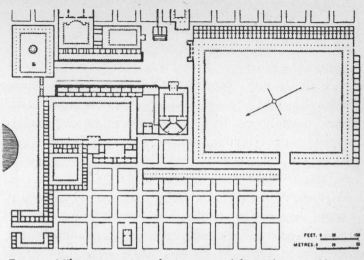

FIG. 23. Miletus, agora, second century A.D. (after *Milet*, i. 2, Abb. 53 ; i. 5, Taf. xlviii, i. 6, Taf. xxvi, and i. 7, Abb. 57)

become a self-contained unit, shut off from the streets and the rest of the town. An impressive example of the peristyle type is the great agora of Ephesus,[26] over 110 m. square, of which the remains are chiefly of Roman imperial date, but it was only one amongst a number of other buildings, some more imposing. When the agora became a mere *building*, however grand, this meant a certain disintegration of the city.

Prevailing tendencies had their effect at Miletus and Magnesia in later Hellenistic and Roman times. At Magnesia columnar gateways were built over the street on the south side. At Miletus the open east side of the large ' horseshoe ' in the north agora was fully built up. The second century A.D. saw a vigorous outburst of building activity ; marked not only by the more complete enclosure of large open areas but also by the excessive and functionless architectural elaboration which had become popular by that time. The south agora was converted into a regular peristyle and provided with a magnificent gateway at the north-east. Near this, facing the Council-House, was built the Nymphaeum, a super-fountain-house. The agora area of Miletus attained its greatest magnificence in the age of Hadrian, but adaptation to prevailing fashions tended to destroy the openness, spaciousness and simplicity of the stoas, and to impair the character of the site as an agora.

In some of the old cities of Greece proper there was a certain tendency to regularize the agora, but it was not carried very far and did not attain the close coordination of the Ionian type. Very long stoas were built along the sides of the agora, defining its roughly rectangular form more clearly. This is what happened at Corinth, as we have seen, at Megalopolis [27] (a new foundation), and most notably at Athens, where a surprising transformation in the appearance and character of the agora in the second century B.C. has been revealed by the excavations (see fig. 24). The stoa of Attalus, extending over 100 m. along the east side, has long been known ; now it appears that this was part of an extensive building scheme. An enormous stoa 150 m. long, at right angles to the Attalus stoa but quite distinct from it, and with an open colonnade all round, was placed across the south part of the agora ; parallel with this a simpler and rather shorter stoa marked the southern limit of the agora.[28] Not much could be done to bring the old buildings strung out along the west side into line with the new elements, but the Metroön at the south end was rebuilt with a colonnade nearly 39 m. long forming a façade

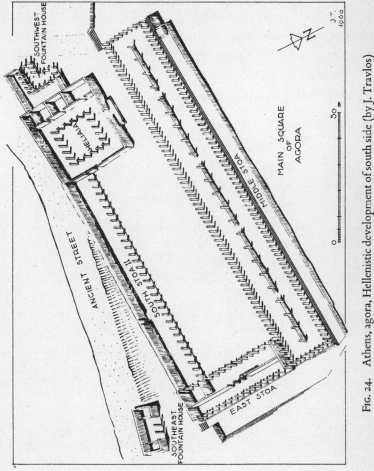

see p. 226

Fig. 24. Athens, agora, Hellenistic development of south side (by J. Travlos)

to a miscellaneous assemblage of rooms and making a slightly acute angle with the peripteral stoa. The agora, or at least part of it, was now something approaching a regular colonnaded square, but it was not Ionian in form, and in fact Pergamene influence is clear. The east stoa is associated with Attalus II of Pergamon ; the types of stoa used have Pergamene parallels and the Metroön, which housed the archives of Athens, is like the library of Pergamon.[29]

V

SHRINES AND OFFICIAL BUILDINGS

HAVING said repeatedly that the temple represents the flower of Greek architecture, I shall not attempt to do it full justice in this work ; I shall merely try to indicate its place, and the place of shrines in general, in the scheme of the city, adding a little about its basic form. This method has some justification when most standard works on Greek architecture rightly allot the greater part of their space to the temple, its growth and the refinements of its classical form, including of course the great orders, which, though they were used in other buildings, were especially associated with the temple.[1]

First of all, one should remember that there is *no* clear line between religious and secular in Greek architecture, any more than in Greek life. The whole city, indeed the whole land, was sacred to the gods, or to some deity in particular — Athens to Athena, Argos to Hera, and so on. The relation could be expressed in various ways ; the god watched over the city ; the city belonged to the god, in a sense it was his shrine, and dedicated to him. The acropolis had its special sanctity, and so had the agora. The streets were associated with Hermes in particular, and at Athens his pillar-like images stood about them in large numbers. The walls had not the rigid sanctity of the Latin *pomerium*, the outer strip of the city ; as we have seen, they formed a looser frame ; but other strips of land might be similarly forbidden to human habitation. Stoas and other public buildings were dedicated to the gods and contained cults with altars and statues. The theatre was the shrine of Dionysus; the gymnasia were attached to various shrines. Finally, in each house the hearth was especially sacred, and an altar often stood in the courtyard too. This universality of the religious element was a very real thing to the Greek; when in time it began to degenerate into something merely formal, and a rift widened between sacred and profane, this meant that something vital in the Hellenic spirit was going.

Various factors tended to make a spot sacred. Physical features excited veneration — caves, groves, hill-tops, springs and streams, the sea. The different centres of human life, both public and private, all had their cults, as we have just seen. The house and hearth of the king were especially sanctified and were succeeded by important temples and the prytaneion with the public hearth. The reputed graves of heroes and founders were hero-shrines; and so were the graves of many historical great men and patriots. Battles and other historical events originated many cults. Sometimes when a new cult was being introduced a place for it had to be chosen quite arbitrarily, and practical convenience and aesthetic considerations decided the matter instead of tradition. On the other hand, some famous shrines were on spots whose sanctity went back to remote pre-Hellenic days. The Greeks scrupulously took them over, installed their own deities, perhaps assigning a niche to their predecessors, and developed the shrines in their own way. Once sacred, a spot clung fast to its sanctity.

'Temple' and 'shrine' are very far from being synonyms. The handsome peripteral temples which we think of as characteristically Greek were luxuries possessed by only a few outstanding shrines amongst all the hundreds which were to be found in any large city. All that was necessary to make a shrine was that a piece of ground or a natural or artificial object should be dedicated to a deity. To preserve the place inviolate the limits had to be defined by simple marks or boundary stones, or more effectively by a fence or wall, making an enclosure. If the cult was to be regularly carried on, an altar was necessary. Altar and boundary were the essentials; an image of the deity *might* be set up, and a temple *might* be built; and in large shrines a great variety of buildings were ultimately added. In classical times shrines of the simplest and most complicated form continued to exist side by side.

In view of their very varied origin and form, it is not surprising that the shrines had no definite place in the structure of the city. They were situated anywhere and everywhere, with certain concentrations, as we have seen, on the acropolis and in the agora. The oldest were older than most of the city itself; the city grew around them and they remained embedded in it; on the other hand, an important shrine sometimes stood at a distance from the city, and was linked with it by a processional way. Ancient shrines could create awkward problems for architects planning ambitious new building schemes. On the Acropolis of Athens the relation of the numerous places of traditional sanctity to the fine new fifth-century buildings required delicate adjustment. The result of such compromises was a curious juxtaposition of antiquated and modern which was very characteristic of Greece. Whether by luck or judgment, the greater temples were very often finely placed. They could hardly fail to be so on the acropolis. Others like the temple of Apollo at Corinth and the 'Theseum' at Athens were placed on lower eminences where they dominated a quarter of the town. These fine effects in the old cities were usually obtained in an informal if not entirely unconscious manner. There was little use of axial planning and other such artificial devices to set off the temples to better advantage. In the agora in particular one does not find a large temple centrally or axially placed so that the agora plays the part of a forecourt. Temples were usually orientated east to west, the east being the main front, but this was not an inviolable rule and could be varied to suit local convenience. The front of the temple was not so strongly emphasized as in the typical Graeco-Roman form. Independent stoas showed some preference for a southern outlook, even when this meant turning their backs on the shrine (see figs. 27 and 28, and Pl. II a).

In Hippodamian towns things were different, but not so radically different as one might expect, or as some ancient writers would have preferred. Aristotle, as we saw, favoured a 'sacred agora'; 'it is fitting', he says (*Politics* vii. 11. 1), 'that the dwellings assigned to the gods . . . should have a suitable site, and *the same for all*'; but with his usual common sense he adds a saving clause — 'excepting those temples which are assigned a special place apart by the law or else by some utterance of the Pythian oracle' (Rackham). Plato (*Laws* 778 c, 779 D) simply advises the concentration of the shrines round the agora, with the government buildings. Xenophon

(*Memorabilia* iii. 8. 10) says that the shrines should be visible to all, but not easily accessible. Pausanias praises the people of Tanagra (ix. 22. 2) because they have their shrines apart from the houses ' in a pure spot away from men '. But these writers and theorists are describing not what *is* normally so but what they think ought to be or what is exceptionally so. Complete segregation of the shrines and precise demarcation of the sacred part of the city was alien to old Greece and was not carried far even by the later planners.

The distribution of the shrines was more or less the same in Hippodamian towns as it had always been, except that the acropolis shed its religious importance too ; where there was one, it was included for reasons of strength, and did not contain the chief temples of the city ; there was no important shrine on the great hill north of Priene. In the lower town the shrines were scattered about as convenience and architectural effect dictated. The difference was that sites could be more deliberately allocated and the orientation of the shrine and its temple was made to conform with the street plan, even when this departed from the usual east-to-west line, as at Miletus. A shrine which was older than the city around it might retain its original orientation in defiance of the new plan, as we saw at Magnesia. One, two or more blocks were allocated to each shrine, and their rectangular form inevitably produced a more uniform type.

The older shrines grew by the piecemeal addition of a variety of buildings, just like the agora, or indeed like the whole city. The greatest shrines of all, the international meeting-places such as Olympia, became in the end veritable cities in themselves — without houses. Between these and the simple enclosure with altar, every intermediate stage continued throughout to be represented. Consider first the original elements. The enclosure might be of any shape, sometimes highly irregular. If the cult grew in importance it would have to be extended, perhaps several times. The enclosing wall varied from a mere formal boundary to a real and powerful fortification, where the shrine was exposed to attack, as at Eleusis. From early archaic times the entrance was commonly adorned with a propylon, the basic form of which was a porch, usually but not always columnar, both inside and outside the actual gateway in the wall. This simple type, which has forerunners in Minoan and Mycenean architecture, could be elaborated by multiplying the columns of the porches and adding wings of various forms. The fifth-century Propylaea of the Athenian Acropolis, for all their apparent complexity, are based on the old propylon. The simplest form of altar was a small mound of earth, or of the ashes of victims. The great altar of Zeus at Olympia remained an ash altar throughout, though it grew to enormous size. Stone altars were made increasingly ornate, until the Hellenistic altars of Zeus at Pergamon, Artemis at Magnesia on the Maeander and Athena at Priene became great works of architecture in themselves, having quite outgrown their proper function and the modest form of the classical altar. When a temple was built the altar was normally in front of it,[2] on the east, and there might also be a subsidiary altar inside for minor sacrifices.

The accompanying plan shows the shrine of Aphaia (a local goddess associated with Artemis) on the island

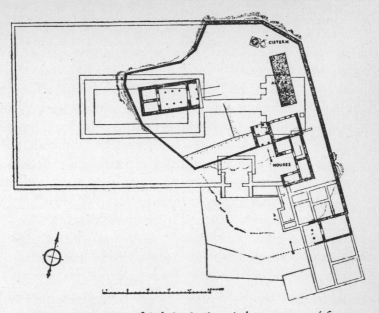

FIG. 25. Sanctuary of Aphaia, Aegina, sixth century B.C. (after
A. Furtwängler, *Aegina*, vol. i, Abb. 402)
The fifth-century reconstruction is shown in outline. The main divisions
on the scale represent five metres

of Aegina at some distance from the city. The cult went
back to early prehistoric times, but the first known
architectural remains are of the seventh century, when
the arrangement of the shrine was probably similar to
what is shown here, but simpler and more restricted in
area. As reconstructed early in the sixth century the
shrine included a temple (the interior arrangement shown
in the plan is partly hypothetical), an altar, an enclosing
wall entered by a propylon, and priests' quarters facing
west over an outer terrace. Early in the fifth century,
probably after being sacked by the Persians, the shrine
was rebuilt on a grander scale, as indicated here in out-

line. The terrace was greatly extended and regularized. A fine new temple, with a colonnade all round, was built, and a large altar to the east, with a paved area for ceremonies in front of it. The subsidiary buildings too were greatly extended. A strongly axial line ran through the temple, a ramp leading up to it from the east, and the altar with its pavement, emphasized by two large bases for groups of statues on either side of the altar ; but this principle was not fully carried out — the enclosure was still not altogether regular and the propylon was placed at right angles to the temple.

Of the buildings acquired by a shrine which attained an imposing architectural form the temple of the main deity was most important but not necessarily first in time ; it might be the culmination of a long process of growth, as at Olympia ; or a long series of temples might succeed one another on the same spot as rebuilding became necessary, each a worthier house for the god than the last ; or else a new temple was built on different ground, and the old retained beside it. Most big shrines contained a number of smaller ones, in which some special cult of the deity was carried on, or a related or subsidiary deity or a hero was worshipped, and these often acquired temples of their own. The ubiquitous stoa had its uses too, and some of the earliest specimens of which remains have been found belong to the shrines of Delos and elsewhere. Priests and officials and the suppliants of the god needed accommodation, and this was provided in the stoas and in house-like buildings sometimes erected round a courtyard. A theatre-like arrangement was needed for some cults, within an enclosed hall if they were ' mysteries '. For other cults, too, special provision

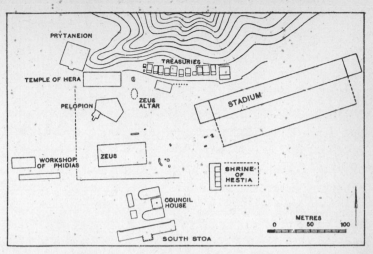

FIG. 26. Olympia, principal monuments in earth fourth century B.C.
(Sketch-plan, after J. D. Kondis, *Olympia in the Fourth Century B.C.*,
Athens, 1958)

had to be made ; for instance, the suppliants of Asclepius
required somewhere to sleep, so that the god could cure
them or reveal a cure in a dream. Shrines such as that
of Asclepius near Epidaurus, the main centre of the cult
of the healing god, and of Aphrodite at Corinth, had
a considerable floating as well as resident population,
while at others the influx was more concentrated at
festival times. But elaborate provision for the convenience and comfort of users of the shrine was mainly
a late development ; arrangements were simple in the
fifth and early fourth century. The sanctuary of Zeus at
Olympia was the greatest religious centre in the Hellenic
world ; but in the fifth century, its greatest days, apart
from the temples (and incidentally Zeus himself did not
acquire a temple till the fifth century) and the ancient
and sacred Prytaneion and Council-House and one or

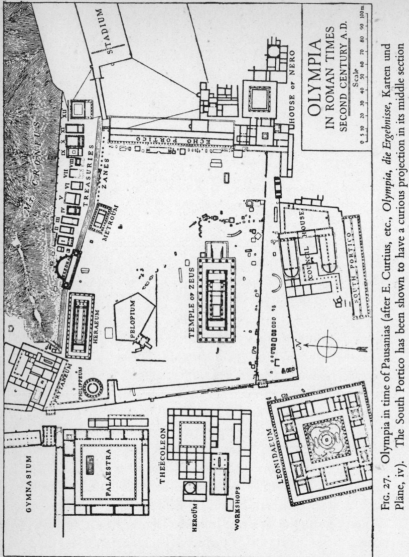

Fig. 27. Olympia in time of Pausanias (after E. Curtius, etc., *Olympia, die Ergebnisse*, Karten und Pläne, iv). The South Portico has been shown to have a curious projection in its middle section

two stoas, there were no large buildings, though there were countless altars and dedicatory statues. In Hellenistic and Roman times a number of magnificent buildings were put up which were devoted rather to the comfort of man than the glory of god, including priests' quarters (the ' Theëkoleon ', a building with two courts), gymnasia and a splendid hotel, the Leonidaion, built round a colonnaded court and surrounded on the outside with colonnades too.

These international shrines were Panhellenic and belonged to the whole Greek world even though attached to a particular city, and drew visitors, especially competitors at the games, from all quarters. They take us beyond the strict limits of our subject, but they were of incalculable importance to the life of the cities, and the present chapter would be incomplete without some reference to them. They required an elaborate organization and developed a correspondingly complex form ; they had many of the administrative and miscellaneous buildings of a large city, and of course stadia for the games and sometimes a theatre. In some of them numerous small temples, the so-called ' treasuries ', were erected by individual cities which vied with one another in honouring the god. Some of these great shrines were several miles distant from the cities with which they were associated (for example, Olympia, the shrine of Asclepius at Epidaurus, and the shrine of Hera at Argos).

The arrangement of the elements in a complex shrine followed no fixed principles. The monuments were scattered about the area in an extremely varied and haphazard way. On some sites an ancient processional way leading from the entrance to the main cult spot had a

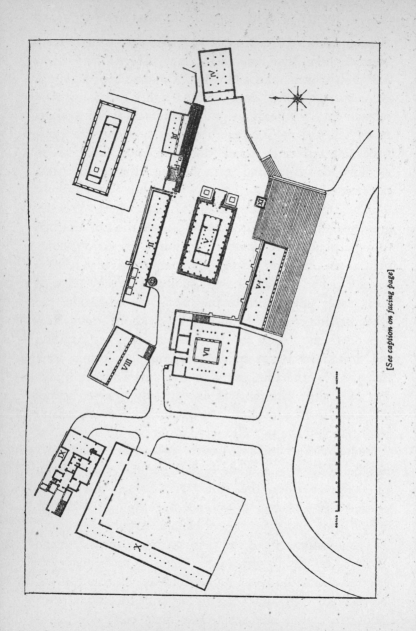

[See caption on facing page]

decisive effect ; [3] the accumulating monuments jostled one another for position along it. The course of the sacred way was usually fixed by tradition and could not be adapted to provide noble vistas of the temple and other buildings. The main temple normally stood approximately in the middle, and the rest of the monuments grouped themselves very informally around. It is difficult for the imagination to picture these shrines correctly, but one can well believe that instinct and informal planning often achieved happy effects ; but the profusion of minor monuments, particularly in the national shrines, must in time have become bewildering and a little wearisome. G. P. Stevens [4] has shown in the case of the Acropolis of Athens, the great shrine of Athena, how, in what now appears to lack coordination, a subtle and effective design may have been at work. The western part, he thinks, was planned along with the Propylaea as a forecourt to the crowning glory of the Acropolis, the Parthenon. It was roughly square and partially

---

Fig. 28. Shrine of Hera near Argos (C. Waldstein, *The Argive Heraeum*, vol. i., Pl. V)

The position and general plan of the buildings are fairly certain, details conjectural

I. Archaic temple (seventh century ; destroyed by fire 423 B.C. and replaced by V).

II, III, VI (see p. 112), VIII. Stoas of sixth and fifth centuries.

IV. East Building (fourth century) ; columnar hall similar to Hall of Mysteries at Eleusis.

V. Later temple (about 420 B.C.).

VII. West Building (sixth century) ; probably a sort of prytaneion, the rooms on either side of the vestibule being dining-halls, rather than a gymnasium or hospital for women suppliants of the goddess, as has been suggested ; see Chap. V, note 31.

IX. Baths of Roman date.

X. L-shaped building of uncertain purpose ; the excavators suggest a court for herding cattle before sacrifice (not very convincing) ; possibly a gymnasium. There were inner supports, but the outer walls are said to be too narrow for column foundations.

The main divisions of the scale represent 5 metres

enclosed by walls ; it was a setting for a number of fine monuments, above all the great bronze Athena of Pheidias, and it allowed fascinating glimpses of the greater wonders beyond. The full beauty of the Parthenon itself, finely placed on a terrace of its own above a broad flight of steps, was not revealed till the visitor had passed through a propylon at the south-east of this court. Possibly further studies of this kind would reveal a more marked design on other sites where monuments seem to have accumulated in a very loose relation to each other. But Stevens admits that the Greeks did not show the same perfection of design in ensembles as in individual buildings. The cumulative effect of a number of buildings, each a masterpiece of proportion and harmony in itself, embedded in a mass of lesser monuments, was apt to be something of a jumble.

Once again Hippodamian planning forcibly imposed order. When one or several rectangular blocks were allotted to a shrine it automatically assumed a regular form. The colonnades were placed in orderly fashion along the sides, sometimes making a complete peristyle. Everything conformed to the prevailing orientation. But even so, a certain amount of freedom was retained, and there was no insistence on strict symmetry about an axis. In the plan of Priene (fig. 6 and fig. 18) it will be observed that the entrance to the shrine of Athena is not placed in the axis of the temple, and in the shrine of Zeus the temple is placed distinctly north of the central line. Highly elaborate axial planning, carried out on a large scale, is characteristic of Roman imperial times ; Baalbek is a striking example, with its entrance portico, hexagonal forecourt and rectangular main court laid out in strict symmetry about the axis of the great temple, and every detail on one side reproduced exactly on the other. Earlier, as von Gerkan points out (p. 105), one does not find the symmetrical alignment of a whole series of architectural motives on the temple axis, though symmetry is preserved in many individual buildings — the temples themselves of course, council-houses, theatres, less commonly gymnasia (*not* houses) ; but in these symmetry was natural, almost inevitable, and enabled the buildings to fulfil their function better.

E. Gjerstad, discussing the origins of the architectural ideas embodied in the imperial fora at Rome (see Ch. IV, n. 26), rightly looks for these to the orient rather than Greece. The ' Kaiserfora ' were built up with strict symmetry about the axis of a temple, which was placed with a strong frontal emphasis at one end of the enclosure. Such methods had some effect in Hellenistic Greece as well as Italy. But Greek planning was by nature freer and more adaptable, and usually less ambitious. Commonsense rather than a fixed architectural idea was the guide. The shrine of Zeus, east of the agora of Priene, is a good example. The temple has a rectangular court with colonnades on either side ; but because the street slopes steeply northward, the modest entrance is pushed as far north as possible. By a kind of attraction the temple and its altar too are pushed north from the centre, but not so far.

The present chapter will provide the best opportunity to say a little more about the relation between sculpture and architecture, a subject which concerns the temples especially though by no means exclusively. In Greece the arts worked in an intimate and mainly harmonious relation with one another and with life in general. One must not think of architecture without its sculptural embellishment, or of sculpture away from its architectural background. The close connection is illustrated by the fact that the same artist was sometimes both sculptor and architect, the younger Polycleitus and Scopas for example ; while Pheidias, primarily a sculptor, had general supervision of the beautification of Athens under Pericles. A great deal of very fine sculpture — the finest that we still have, in fact, belongs to this class — formed a decorative incrustation for the temples, and to a much smaller extent for other buildings. The artists realized unerringly how, where and to what extent they could best apply this decoration so as to enhance the severe beauty of the Doric order or the lighter grace of the Ionic, without blurring it or distracting the eye. Pediments, metopes (Doric) and frieze (not so exclusively Ionic as is sometimes imagined) were the main fields, and sculptured *acroteria* were placed at the corners of the gables. It was felt that to decorate the structurally most vital parts with sculpture would give a sense of weakness, but in one or two exceptional cases the lower drums of columns (temple of Artemis at Ephesus) and the architrave (archaic temple at Assos) were carved in relief. Apart from this specifically architectural sculpture, the temple normally housed a cult image (but not always) which might be a crude figure of early archaic date or a colossal and gorgeous creation in gold and ivory, itself lavishly encrusted in minor sculptural decoration. The larger temples tended to become great museums of art ; the Greeks could dispense with museums and art galleries as such since art was everywhere. Statues

were placed in the colonnades, in the front and back
porch, and along the sides of the cella itself, or flanking
the chief cult statue ; the temples also contained objects
which were curious rather than beautiful. Pausanias
offers plentiful illustrations ; take the temple of Athena
Alea at Tegea, which he thought the finest in Pelopon-
nesus (viii. 45. 4 ff.). The pedimental sculptures represented the Calydonian boar-hunt and a fight in the
Trojan War, and the altar had reliefs of Rhea with the
baby Zeus and a number of nymphs ; amongst the
contents of the temple, besides the image of Athena,
flanked by Asclepius and Health, Pausanias singles out
as ' most notable ' the tusks and hide of the Calydonian
boar, fetters worn by Spartan prisoners, the sacred couch
of Athena, a painting of Auge, and the shield of Marpessa,
a valorous lady of Tegea.

Such collections naturally had little artistic unity.
On the other hand, in a few masterpieces of combined
architecture and sculpture — and painting too — the
carved and painted decoration formed a single scheme,
one in artistic design and one in meaning. The Parthenon
is the supreme example. The east pediment showed
the birth of Athena, with the goddess recently sprung
from the head of Zeus and now fully grown and fully
armed ; the west showed Athena and Poseidon contend-
ing for the land of Attica by producing gifts in rivalry.
On the metopes were carved legendary battles, of gods
and giants, heroes and centaurs, and others. The frieze
showed the Panathenaic procession, with the flower of
the Athenian people coming to do homage to their
goddess. Inside the temple was the great gold and ivory
statue of Athena Parthenos, and some of the themes of

the exterior sculpture were taken up and emphasized in the subsidiary decoration of the cult image. Pheidias, who designed the whole, had made skilful use of the traditional mythological subjects of art (except in the frieze) to give a grand impression of the creation of the Hellenic and Attic spirit, its enrichment by the gods, its triumph over barbarous enemies, and its final flowering in the Athens of Pericles.

Pausanias saw famous paintings in the shrines too, for example, in the Theseum at Athens (i. 17. 2) and on the screens enclosing the throne of Zeus at Olympia (v. 11. 4). Painting too was related to architecture, though not so obviously or closely. The walls of certain stoas were decorated with great pictures, as we shall see. Most famous of all was the Lesche (lounge or club-room, x. 25 ff.) of the Cnidians at Delphi, a rectangular building with the door in the middle of one long side, on whose walls Polygnotus painted his masterpieces, the Fall of Troy and Odysseus in the Underworld. Of course, decorative architectural detail too was picked out in colour, but this is a different matter.

Besides the works of art which formed part of the decoration or contents of temples and other buildings, others too which stood more or less independently must not be dissociated from their architectural setting. In the shrines they accumulated mainly along the sacred way and opposite the main front of the temple. If the accumulation became too great for the space available, as happened particularly in the national shrines, the minor works ended by conflicting with or obscuring the aims of the architects. In addition to the aesthetically unfortunate congestion, one finds such tragi-comic situations

as a monument of an Arcadian victory over Sparta right
in front of a monument of a Spartan victory over Athens,
and a gilded statue of a courtesan near the tripod which
commemorated the great victory of Greeks over Persians
at Plataea — all these seen by Pausanias at Delphi (x.
9. 5, 7-10 ; 13. 9 ; 15. 1).

The Greek temple was a house, the house of a god,
or at least it represented the main hall of a house. It
was the expression of an essentially anthropomorphic
religion, and the desire to provide an appropriate setting
for a cult statue was an important factor in determining
its form. The temple was not intended to house large
gatherings of worshippers ; the open shrine outside was
used for this purpose, though for certain cults a special
hall was provided, such as the Telesterion or hall of
mysteries at Eleusis, built on quite a different principle
from the temple ; the theatre too was a specialized form
of meeting-place for a large congregation.

The basic form of the temple was an oblong building
with the entrance at one end. This is the so-called
megaron form which, brought down originally from the
north in pre-Hellenic times, recurred in age after age
in Greece, and of which more will be said in dealing with
the house (see p. 180). It normally had an open entrance
porch or occasionally an antechamber, though some
early temples were plain rectangles ; sometimes there
was a small room at the rear which formed an inner
sanctum. The entrance porch, the depth of which
varied greatly, was usually adorned with columns, either
between forward continuations of the side walls (*in antis*)
or in front (*prostyle*) ; a similar porch might be added
at the rear for the sake of symmetry, not normally giving

entrance to the building. The interior of large temples was divided longitudinally by rows of columns, for structural or decorative effect, or both ; in a number of mainly archaic examples there was a single row ; but this arrangement had obvious disadvantages for the setting of the cult statue, and usually there were two rows, marking off side aisles which were occasionally made into a series of side chapels by short walls joining the columns to the main walls.[5] More rarely a peristyle effect was obtained by continuing the columns round the back end.

The most revolutionary development was, of course, the addition of an external colonnade completely enveloping the nuclear building. This is not to be thought of as a mere extension of the colonnades of the porches round the sides. It was introduced very early and is found in a curious hairpin-shaped form in one of the earliest known temples, at Thermon in Aetolia in northwest Greece ; and it seems to have been placed over the whole building at once as a protective and decorative frame. It was placed around all types of inner structure, including those which had columnar porches in any case. Sometimes already existing temples were provided with a colonnade, drastic rebuilding being necessary. The columns were carried to the full height of the temple, so that its original nature was masked and a complete transformation effected *outwardly*. Equipped with its colonnade the temple was more than ever marked out as the city's chief architectural adornment ; unlike the house, and indeed unlike all other early Greek buildings, it presented an imposing façade on every side.

In all its essentials, including the outer colonnade,

the temple may be regarded as a *Greek* product, owing nothing to foreign importations ; we can see it growing from the crudest beginnings. 'To Egyptian and oriental influence it owed merely decorative detail and a tendency towards greater elaboration and magnificence (and, to some extent, the replacement of wood and clay by stone). This is not the place to speak of the origin of details of the orders, though I believe that Doric at least was almost wholly native ; but in the colossal Ionic temples of the sixth century the multiplication of columns, including the duplication of the outer colonnade, and the general elaboration show foreign influence (cf. Pl. VIII (*b*)). An important variant on the double colonnade was achieved by placing a *single* colonnade in the position in which the outer row would be in the double scheme.

The temple made rapid strides in early archaic times, leaving all other building types well behind. 'In our period', Weickert says,[6] 'only real cult-buildings were monumental, everything else was comparatively simple' ; also, 'building is for these men just as much the service of god as making a statue'. By the beginning of the sixth century, as the Heraeum of Olympia shows in spite of its construction of wood and unbaked brick on a stone socle (fig. 27), the temple was complete in essentials of plan. The Heraeum had a *cella*, or main room, with internal columns (some of them engaged in cross-walls) along the sides and a columnar porch at either end, and a complete external colonnade ; this became the prevalent form for the greatest temples, and even the fifth century could add nothing fundamentally new. What was left for the sixth- and fifth-century architects was to complete the adjustments made necessary by the transition from the early wooden construction to stone, adapting certain features of the former as decorative motives ; to find by experiment the ideal design and proportions for the whole building and for individual members ; and to weld the parts into a perfect unity, overcoming the original awkwardness which was experienced in applying the outer colonnade to the inner structure. As a result the temple took on a new strength and beauty, enhanced by the increasing use of fine marbles in place of limestone.

Simple forms of plan were retained alongside the more elaborate in later archaic and classical times. A rectangular cella with a columnar porch was a common type of small temple. Early curvilinear forms long survived in buildings in which the rear end curved into an apse ; on the other hand, the circular shrine, of which we have several notable examples, is probably not to be thought of as the lineal descendant of the primitive circular hut ; the most important classical *tholoi*, or round buildings, such as those of Delphi and Epidaurus, are exquisite and highly sophisticated creations, with nothing of the archaic about them, and in fact advanced in their internal use of experimental forms of the new Corinthian order.

The size of the temples varied enormously, from little gems like the temple of Athena Nike on the Acropolis of Athens (about $18\frac{1}{2}$ by 27 ft.) to giants just about a thousand times as big, like the temple of Zeus at Acragas (over 180 by 380 ft.), of which there were only about half a dozen in the Greek world. Most important cities possessed several large temples, not indeed on this colossal scale, but sufficiently grand to play a dominant rôle in the city's architectural form.

The basic rectangular form, with entrance at one end and varying degrees of external and internal columnar embellishment, prevailed almost universally. There were a few squarish temples and a very few placed crosswise with the entrance on one of the long sides (occasionally a cella of normal form had an additional side door). Where variations and complications occur, they are usually due to the peculiar requirements of cult, though here and there one feels that the architect was deliberately experimenting, for example, in the temple of Apollo at Bassae with its side entrance and other peculiar features, and the huge temple of Olympian Zeus at Acragas in Sicily, in which the outer columns were built into a continuous wall. Sometimes two cults had to be housed in one temple, and one was accommodated in an outer room, one in an inner (Pausanias ii. 10. 2, vi. 20. 3), or one in a cella facing east, the other in another facing west (ii. 25. 1, viii. 9. 1). An extreme example of complication is the Erechtheum at Athens, with its main room facing east and two small rooms behind a large ante-room facing west, and a large porch on the north and a small one on the south unsymmetrically placed, not to speak of a crypt, a rare feature. The whole building managed to embrace a number of curious cults and sacred spots, and yet others adjoined it. But the Erechtheum was a quite exceptional building. Most Greek temples were simple and compact. Several large temples, including one or two of the colossal two-colonnaded buildings, were exceptional in another way ; the cella was not roofed over, so that it formed a court-yard rather than a room, and in some cases a small temple

was built within it to house the cult statue ; [7] in fact
the main structure had quite outgrown its proper function ; there is something foreign to the spirit of the
native Greek temple in this unwieldy growth.

To pass on to buildings whose function was not primarily religious, though they still cannot be distinguished
as entirely secular — the stoa [8] was an architectural type
of first-rate importance. It was an all-purpose building,
and played a vital part in Greek architecture and Greek
life. The Athenian orators constantly include the stoas
among the glories of the city ; Demosthenes couples
them with the masterpieces of the Acropolis, the Propylaea and the Parthenon, and with the ship-sheds [9] of
Peiraeus (xxii. 76, xxiii. 207, etc.). Like ' agora ' the
Greek word is untranslatable, and I shall use it in preference to ' portico ' or ' colonnade '.

The stoa was in essentials a very simple and adaptable building, consisting merely of an open colonnade,
normally with a back wall, to which the columns were
joined by a roof. Such a structure had many architectural uses ; it could form an entrance porch, or a
façade ; it could be placed on one or more sides of a
court and could form an internal or external peristyle.
All these uses are dependent ; but the stoa could also
be an independent architectural unit, and it is with this
use that we shall be mainly concerned, though the word
embraces the others too. Colonnades have of course
been used to good practical and artistic effect in many
ages and lands ; for instance, among the forerunners of
Greek architecture, by the Egyptians in magnificent
temple courts and by the Minoans and Myceneans in

palaces. The colonnade as an independent free-standing unit is especially characteristic of the Hellenic cities.

The prominence of the stoa in Greek architecture is easily explained. It suited the climate of Greece, offering welcome shade from the heat and ready shelter from wind and squalls; it was easily adaptable to a variety of purposes in public life and possessed great artistic possibilities. Its origin and early growth are more obscure. One remote ancestor may perhaps be found in the colonnades of the Mycenean palace courtyard, which sometimes give the impression of being detached units rather than a compact peristyle. Possibly this type of structure was not entirely lost in the house architecture of the dark ages, and as the city was taking shape the idea of equipping public places and shrines similarly may have given rise to the independent stoa; in the agora, especially, it provided the ordinary citizen with a pleasant sheltered place in which to do business or take his ease. Or again, flimsy but useful lean-to shelters or booths may have suggested something more permanent and handsome; sometimes a light colonnade was placed against an already existing wall, as in an archaic example from the shrine of Hera at Samos [10] and in the stoa of the Athenians at Delphi (early fifth century; Pl. IX), which used the great polygonal retaining wall as a backing; here we have another possible line of development for the stoa. In any case, one may claim once more that the stoa is an artistic form created by Greek inventive genius out of simple elements to satisfy real needs.[11]

Early remains are scanty, obscure and difficult to date, and are mostly associated with shrines; Delos had several. By the fifth century the stoa was counted among the notable features of many cities, and of the agora in particular. Most large stoas had an inner row of columns to give them greater spaciousness and dignity. Frequently when the main order of the building was Doric the inner columns were Ionic,[12] just as Ionic columns were used in the rear chamber of the Parthenon and the interior of other Doric buildings; the inner columns were usually twice as widely spaced as the outer. The south stoa of the Argive Heraeum (fifth century; one of an interesting series in the shrine, see fig. 28, vi) is a clear example of the simple two-aisled stoa. A few large stoas had two rows of inner supports (one of the large stoas at Elis, and later the stoa of Philip at Megalopolis). In the other stoa at Elis a colonnade was built on either side of a central wall; and at Delos and elsewhere there were other stoas placed back to back. The ends consisted of walls returning at right angles to the back wall and either extending to the front of the building or stopping short to leave place for the end columns; or alternatively of short colonnades. Sometimes the colonnade did not extend along the whole of the front and there were sections of solid wall at either end (occasionally one end only).[13] In this case the stoa tended to approximate to an enclosed hall. The great Hellenistic Hypostyle Hall at Delos presented a façade of this type; inside it was more than a stoa, being in fact a multi-columnar hall of the kind of which we shall have something to say in the next section. L-shaped or obtuse-angled stoas occur even in archaic times and continue to be used; the more elaborate right-angled schemes come later.

There is something architecturally unsatisfying about

FIG. 29. Heraeum at Samos, reconstruction of South Stoa (Ath. Mit., lxxxii, 1957, Tafel VII)

a long colonnade which simply comes to an end without anything to define its form or concentrate its artistic interest. To produce a more finished and satisfying unit, shallow projecting wings were added at either end, surmounted by gables. The effect can best be seen in the stoa of Zeus (Royal Stoa ?) at Athens, which, built in the latter part of the fifth century, was perhaps the prototype of this form. The building has been accurately reconstructed from foundations and fragments of the superstructure ; it was about 45 m. long and 12 m. wide in the middle, 18 m. at the wings. The main order was Doric, the inner columns Ionic. The central part had its columns more widely spaced than those of the wings, and thus had the advantage of greater open-ness. The floor may have been paved with stone but this is not clear. Just inside the foundations of the walls are traces of benches. Sculptural decoration was con-fined to the acroteria on the pediments of the wings, but a number of important monuments stood in front of the central colonnade. Two rooms which formed an annexe behind were not added till much later (see fig. 13).

This building deserves special notice because it belongs to the finest period of Athenian architecture, and because it represents the ideal form of a single independent stoa and stands at the head of a whole series. H. A. Thompson [14] thinks that the creation of a satisfying design by the addition of wings may be compared to the way in which the old type of columnar gateway was elaborated in the Propylaea of the Athenian Acropolis, which were built a little earlier ; but the wings of the Propylaea were bigger and not so compactly joined to the main structure. However, it is certainly true that the scheme with balancing wings became popular from this time, in stoas, in entrance porticoes, and in the stage-building of the theatre, whose projecting wings were called *paraskenia*. In one or two buildings of similar plan to the stoa of Zeus the wings seem to have been not open porches but enclosed by walls ; there is a building of this type in the agora of Thasos (late fourth century, see fig. 2). In the stoa of Philip at Megalopolis (fourth century, though the exist-

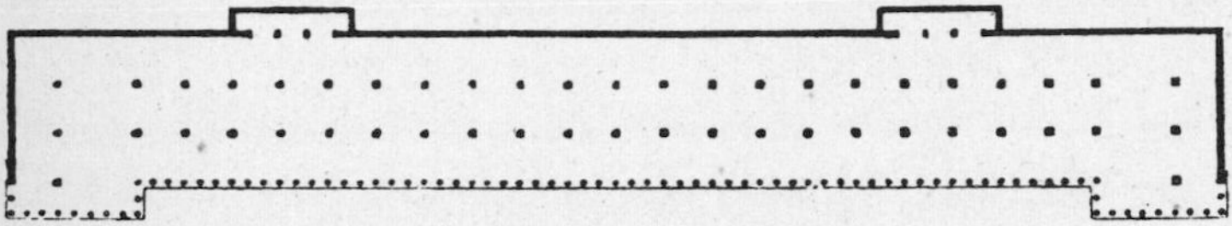

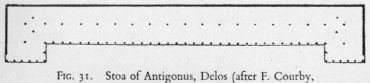

FIG. 30. Stoa of Philip, Megalopolis (after E. A. Gardner, etc., *Excavations at Megalopolis*)

FIG. 31. Stoa of Antigonus, Delos (after F. Courby, *Le Portique d'Antigone, Délos*, v)

ing remains are probably second century and the original form is not certain) and the stoa of Antigonus at Delos (third century), the winged form is carried out on a huge scale — the first was 156 m. long, the second 120 m. — but the actual projection of the wings is not increased in proportion to the size of the building. The stoa of Philip had a double row of interior columns. There was an increasing tendency in the fourth century and the Hellenistic age to build stoas of enormous length ; the fact that the great corn storehouse built under Pericles in Peiraeus was distinguished as the Long Stoa (there was also a Long Stoa in Athens itself) implies that there was something exceptional about it in the fifth century.

We have already discussed the ' horseshoe ' and other ways of laying out stoas in rectangular schemes ; one might add, however, that the ' horseshoe ' can hardly be considered the result of an extension of projecting wings. The wings of the stoa of Zeus are not much more than ornamental terminations, and face the same way as the central colonnade. The sides of the ' horseshoe ' have their façades at right angles to the central part, and are stoas in themselves. Magnesia in particular (fig. 19) will make the difference plain. The two types may approximate but in principle they are very different, and the ' horseshoe ' may best be regarded as an invention of Ionian architects ; it *may* have been suggested by the older L-shaped stoas.

In the Hellenistic age new and magnificent forms were invented or developed, especially in the Pergamene sphere. Two-storeyed colonnades, rare but not unknown earlier, were very much favoured at Pergamon. The upper colonnade formed a gallery over the lower and

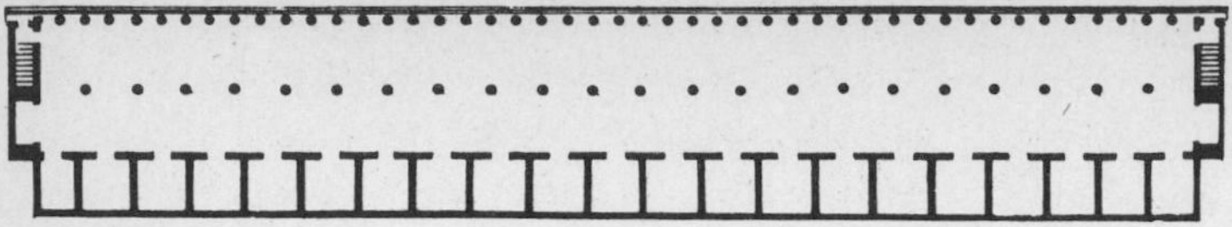

FIG. 32. Stoa of Attalus, Athens (by J. Travlos)

its columns were joined by a balustrade. The best example of the type is the huge stoa built in the agora at Athens through the generosity of Attalus II of Pergamon. After a slight extension it was about 116 m. long, and each floor consisted of a great hall with a row of twenty-one shops behind. This great market-hall is far removed from the booths of the early agora, and even from the simplicity of the classic stoas.

Inspired by the necessities and opportunities which met them in dealing with steeply sloping sites, the Hellenistic architects — again largely Pergamene — went even further in ingenuity by giving the stoa elaborate substructures. The colonnade opened on to the agora-terrace, but the other side of the building, facing down the slope, included not only the back of the colonnade but also several lower storeys. The best examples are not at Pergamon itself but at Aegae, Alinda and Assos.[15] The

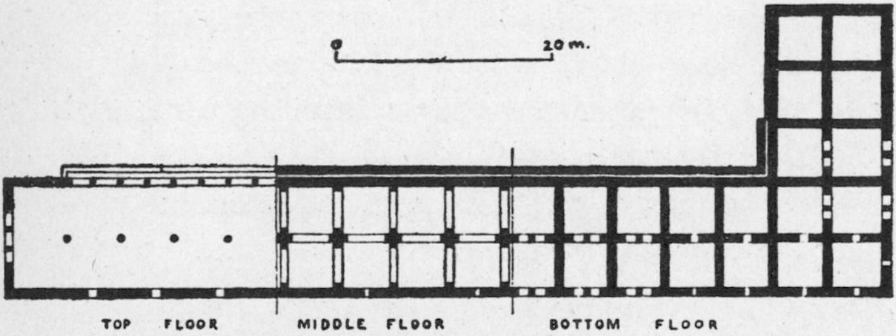

20 m.

TOP FLOOR MIDDLE FLOOR BOTTOM FLOOR

FIG. 33. Market-building, Aegae (R. Bohn, *Altertümer von Aegae*, Abb. 16)

Aegae example is over 80 m. long, with a short wing.
The back is formed by a huge wall of three storeys,
broken by windows and in the lowest storey by doors ;
the front was a colonnade opening on to the agora,
which was at the level of the top storey. The plan
shows how each floor was divided. With these huge
market-halls the history of the form of the stoa may be
concluded. One may indeed doubt whether they can
reasonably be called stoas at all, since the colonnade
merely crowns the more substantial elements below ;
but at least they grew out of the stoa, by the addition
of substructures on a sloping terraced site.

The stoas were used for purposes as varied as the
agora itself. They were of course by no means confined
to the agora, but were to be found everywhere ; on the
streets, especially those leading to the agora, such as the
dromos at Athens which led to the main gate, the Dipylon, though long completely colonnaded streets belong
to a later age ; in all shrines which had any claim to
architectural elaboration ; and in gymnasia — at Aegium,
Pausanias says (vii. 23. 5), a stoa was specially built
for Straton the pancratiast to practise in, and covered
running-tracks often took the form of stoas ; the theatre
too sometimes had a stoa attached to it giving convenient
shelter to the audience.

In the agora the stoas had all sorts of political, commercial and general functions. They could house a
meeting of the council or of a court of law, provide
headquarters for magistrates and contain official documents. Business men too used them. The rooms
opening on them served as offices or shops and store-
rooms. The North Building at Corinth [16] provides a

fifth-century example of the latter; its shops had counters next to the doors, and tanks lined with cement — the building was probably a fish-market. Goods were stored in the stoas, and samples were set out for inspection in stoas called *deigmata*. We have already come across examples of most of these uses. The walls were sometimes decorated with great paintings and the building took on the character of a picture-gallery, though not reserved exclusively for this purpose. Subjects for painting and sculpture were naturally chosen from glorious episodes in the city's history, legendary or real, and this made halls of victory of the Poikile at Athens and the Persian Stoa at Sparta, which was built from spoils of the Persian War and decorated with figures of Persians (Pausanias i. 15. 1, iii. 11. 3). The adaptability of the stoa is best seen in the Royal Stoa and the Poikile at Athens. The former was so called because it was the seat of the Archon Basileus who inherited the religious functions of the old kings; it was also used on occasion for meetings of the august court of the Areopagus; in it stood copies of the laws of Solon, inscribed on stone pillars, along with other important inscriptions; and it was used by merchants and the general public. Finally, it was a picture-gallery too, if Thompson is right in thinking that the stoa of Zeus and the Royal are identical. The Poikile, on the other hand, was chiefly famous for its pictures, which were painted by the greatest artists, and ranged from Theseus and the Amazons and the Trojan War to Marathon and a fight against the Spartans (captured Spartan shields were also displayed, and one of these has been found). But the stoa was used for trade and recreation too, and occasionally as a court-room. Many philosophical discussions must have taken place here such as the very lively example described by Lucian (*Zeus Trag.* 16), and Zeno adopted the place in the latter part of the fourth century ; that is why his school was called Stoic. Thus a word whose proper meaning is architectural has been taken over in modern languages in a philosophical and moral sense.

The stoa was an excellent building for general social purposes, and a useful and decorative adjunct to any public place, but for some of its more specialized functions it was not so well adapted. It was not an ideal court- or council-room, and we do not know how the seating was arranged when it was used for these purposes. The Greeks eventually created a distinctive and practical type of enclosed and covered meeting-place for a deliberative body of several hundreds, though their early efforts were very varied and tentative.[17]

The general assembly of the whole citizen body of a large state was a different matter. Originally the citizens had gathered in the open agora, and perhaps in some towns they continued to do so. Little more than a platform for the orators was needed for an assembly place, and some simple kind of standing or sitting accommodation, preferably in roughly theatral form. The theatre was in origin associated with the assembly-place, and when fully developed as a distinct building, though designed for dramatic festivals, it was often found to be the best place for large political gatherings too. Evidence on the subject is very imperfect, but it is at least doubtful whether many cities possessed, like Athens with its Pnyx, a building specially designed for a very large assembly, in addition to the theatre. *Roofed* buildings for a gathering of several thousands were rare indeed ; the limitations of constructional technique created difficulties ; a forest of internal columns, the only means by which a vast roof could be supported, was hardly an advantage in an assembly-hall. The Greeks had nothing to equal the basilicas and other great vaulted or domed structures of the Romans. But in any case the need for such halls was not normally felt ; open-air assembly-places sufficed. A building such as the Thersilion at Megalopolis was an exceptional *tour de force*.

The Athenian Pnyx deserves special notice ; it was a highly individual building with a unique history, yet at the same time it probably embodied the main principle of the majority of Greek assembly-places ; and a few years ago it was the subject of a careful investigation by H. A. Thompson,[18] with surprising results, which show that the familiar rock-cut scarp and platform actually belong to a late rearrangement. In spite of drastic changes the principle remained throughout that of the theatre, with auditorium sloping down to and focused upon the place where the speakers stood. The Pnyx was a short distance to the south-west of the classical Agora of Athens, but the slope on which it was built rose immediately above the site of the presumed older agora. As Thompson remarks, if a quieter and roomier spot than the agora itself was required, this slope was the obvious place to choose. At first the natural hillside was used, with perhaps a platform for the speakers at its foot. Late in the sixth century the rock was dressed in the upper part of the auditorium, and at the bottom a retaining wall was built, supporting a terrace. There was accommodation for about 5000,

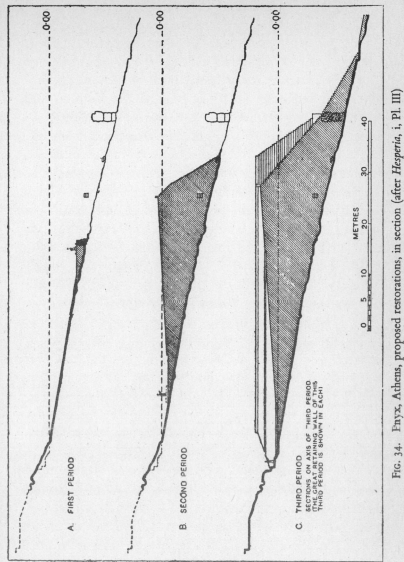

A. FIRST PERIOD

B. SECOND PERIOD

C. THIRD PERIOD

SECTIONS ON AXIS OF "THIRD PERIOD"
(THE GREAT RETAINING WALL OF THIS
THIRD PERIOD IS SHOWN IN EACH)

METRES

0   5   10   20   30   40

Fig. 34. Pnyx, Athens, proposed restorations, in section (after *Hesperia*, i, Pl. III)

without artificial seating. About a century later (towards 400 B.C.) the whole building was turned round, so that the natural slope led *down* from the *bema* or speaker's platform towards the back of the auditorium. A curved retaining wall was built at the bottom, and within this a great embankment was raised in order to give the auditorium a slight upward slope from the bema. The motive for this curious reversal is obscure ; it gave the building greater seclusion and a south-westerly instead of a north-easterly outlook, but even so Greek architects seldom went so strongly against nature in such buildings. There were still no seats except perhaps wooden benches ; the main entrances were two stairways at the back. The final reconstruction, which Thompson now attributes to Lycurgus [19] in the fourth century instead of a Hadrianic revival (second century A.D.) as he first thought, was an extension of this scheme in all directions. The stronger retaining wall which is still conspicuous was made, and at the top the rock was cut into a scarp with the present bema projecting from it. The Pnyx would now hold 10,000 people ; still no permanent stone seating was provided ; the entrance was by stairs rising over the back wall, leading up from the direction of the agora.

The Pnyx was not without rivals as an assembly place at Athens ; even in the fifth century the Assembly sometimes gathered elsewhere ; for example, ostracisms were held down in the agora itself, in the *perischoinisma* (*i.e.* ' a place roped off '). From the middle of the fourth century the theatre, where the first meeting after the great dramatic festival had been held even earlier, was used more frequently ; and in the third and second centuries meetings at Peiraeus, hitherto exceptional, became more common.

The Spartan assembly [20] met in a building called the Skias (Canopy) which stood where a road left the agora, and though attributed locally to Theodorus of Samos (sixth century B.C.), was still used in Pausanias' time (iii. 12. 10). The name implies a roof, but the construction of the building is not known. The most striking example of a roofed assembly-place is the Thersilion at Megalopolis (Pl. X), which was built soon after 371 B.C. for the Ten Thousand, the federal assembly of the newly founded Arcadian state. Pausanias (viii. 32. 1) calls the Thersilion a council-house (*bouleuterion*) ; and it cannot be altogether separated in function and principles of construction from the buildings which will be dealt with in the next section. What distinguishes it is its size ; the Megalopolitans had their own small council-house in their agora, on the opposite bank of the river Helisson. The Thersilion was a valiant attempt to enclose with a roof and four walls an area which if left unroofed would have been rather like the embankment of the Pnyx. The floor was like a very shallow theatre, sloping gently down from north, east and west to a flat space near the middle of the south side. Curiously, the slope is against the contours once more — it goes downwards away from the river bed. The nature of the seating is uncertain. The walls measured 218 ft. (E.–W.) by 172 ft. The columns which supported the roof were cunningly placed so that they stood not only in concentric rectangles but also on radial lines drawn from the central space. This arrangement was less obstructive to the view than that of most other Greek hypostyle halls, such as the Hall of Mysteries at Eleusis.[21] A long columnar porch was added to the middle part of the south side. The building was typical of the grandiosity of Megalopolis; and adjoining it on the south was built the largest theatre in Greece, in which the Ten Thousand could listen to their orators without any craning of necks around columns.

The assemblies of most federal leagues met in a shrine where they maintained some traditional cult in common, and the evidence, or lack of it, seems to show that not many of them had a special building for the purpose. However, Pausanias describes another interesting specimen, the Phokikon at Daulis, where the Phocians met. It was of huge size, says Pausanias (x. 5. 1), and inside were columns standing along its length, presumably two rows dividing the building into three aisles. From the columns tiers of seats rose to each side wall.[22] This is different from the usual theatre principle, though one might regard the two sides as two flat theatres facing one another; and again the view cannot have been very good for all. But again, such a building was exceptional. Most great assemblies met under the sky. The opening scene of Aristophanes' *Acharnians* gives a characteristic glimpse; Dicaeopolis is shown sitting in the Pnyx, looking out over the city to his beloved Attic countryside beyond. The orators could point to the land and the sea from which the greatness of Athens rose, and to the gleaming marble temples which were its most conspicuous symbol. This was the setting in which the liveliest of all political assemblies met; closer confinement would have been unnatural. It was similar in the theatre; the audience, especially in the back rows, could look out over the Attic plain to the mountains and the sea, and behind them towered the Acropolis ; this was the right setting for the Assembly and for the drama which sprang from the soil of Attica ; to enclose the building with high walls and to put a roof on it would have destroyed its spirit.

However, one still cannot draw a definite line between buildings intended for a general assembly and the bouleuterion which was normally roofed. If the Thersilion could be called a bouleuterion, a small well-designed hall at Priene has been rightly labelled *ekklesiasterion* or assembly-hall because it was big enough to hold the whole citizen body of the little town, though it must have housed the council too, and may also have been used as a law-court.

From the beginning the council-house was an enclosed building. It took over the tradition of the king's council-chamber, in which he consulted his chiefs. Thus it shared with the prytaneion the inheritance left by the royal halls ; the close kinship of the two is shown by the fact that though the prytaneion contained the sacred hearth of the city, the council-house too often had an altar of Hestia, goddess of the hearth. As the cities developed politically, democratically elected councils required a dignified hall where they could deliberate in seclusion no less than their regal and aristocratic predecessors.

In many cities the council-house must have been amongst the earliest public buildings ; but the most interesting specimen of an archaic council-house comes from Olympia, one of the great national sanctuaries which, as we saw, contained the usual administrative

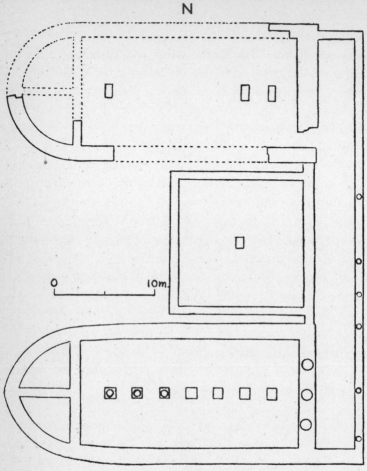

N

0 _____ 10m.

S

FIG. 35. Council-House, Olympia (after E. N. Gardiner, *Olympia*, fig. 115 ; Curtius and Adler, *Olympia*, i. 55)

offices. Great antiquity and piecemeal growth account
for its very peculiar form. Two hair-pin shaped buildings stood parallel, with a square room or enclosure
between them. The north wing was probably built in
the sixth century and the south early in the fifth, but the
latter preserves a more primitive plan, since its walls
curve slightly along the whole of their length, whereas
those of the north wing are straight except for the apse.
The square structure, with the colonnade on the front
uniting all three, was not added till the third century.
The wings each had a single row of interior supports.
The identification of the whole complex as council-
house is practically certain, but the purpose of the
various parts is obscure ; probably the oblong rooms were
council-chambers proper (or perhaps only one of them
was), and the small rooms in the apses were offices or
archive rooms ; and the central square was possibly an
open shrine.[23] But in any case it is clear that an ancient
architectural tradition was the decisive factor rather than
practical convenience.

Delphi too had an archaic council-house, a longish
rectangular building about 6 m. by 13 m. This oblong
form was far from ideal, but it continued to be used
in a few places. Even when a compact and convenient
design had been evolved and was in general use, the
type was not altogether fixed. Hence identification is
often difficult ; remains of council-houses are not
always recognizable beyond dispute ; and a number of
nondescript rectangular buildings, appropriately situated,
have been labelled as council-houses. With such uncertain material it is very easy to argue in circles about
the form of the bouleuterion. Long stoas were used, as

we have seen, including, probably, two winged stoas of fourth-century date at Mantinea and Calauria.

The form which ultimately prevailed, almost to the exclusion of these indeterminate types, was achieved by placing a small theatre-like arrangement inside a squarish hall. Improved roofing technique helped. If Thompson's reconstructions of the Council-Houses of Athens are correct, it now appears that this type, of which the best and clearest examples are Hellenistic, was already established in the fifth century, and its beginnings even go back to the sixth. The older Athenian Council-House (late sixth century ; see fig. 12) was nearly square (23·3 m. by 23·8 m.), but a large section was cut off on the south to form a vestibule. The position of the interior supports is fairly clear from the remains, but the restoration of the seating (no doubt wooden) is merely

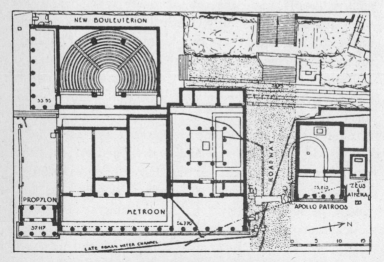

FIG. 36. Athens, Council-House and adjacent buildings
(part of *Hesperia*, vi, p. 397, fig. 1)

PLATE I

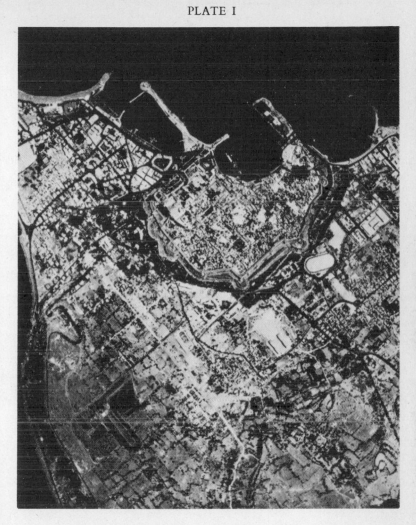

Rhodes, air view (*photo*, supplied by Mr. I. D. Kondis)

The mediaeval and modern town clusters around the main (central) harbour. The ancient city occupied most of the peninsula here visible. Traces of its grid are preserved in many streets and field-boundaries. The agora was probably near the harbour. Mt. Smith, on the west, formed an acropolis, with the temple of Athena and Zeus (north of the stadium). See p. 23 and Ch. II supplementary n. 1.

PLATE II

(a) Priene, central part as from south-east, model by H. Schleif in Pergamon Museum, Berlin

(b) Sacred Stoa, Priene (restoration, from M. Schede, *Die Ruinen von Priene*)

PLATE III

(a) Panakton (Gyphtokastro), fourth-century Attic border fort
(*photo*, Hellenic Society)

(b) Messene, section of fourth-century wall and Arcadian Gate
(*photo*, Deutscher Kunstverlag)

PLATE IV

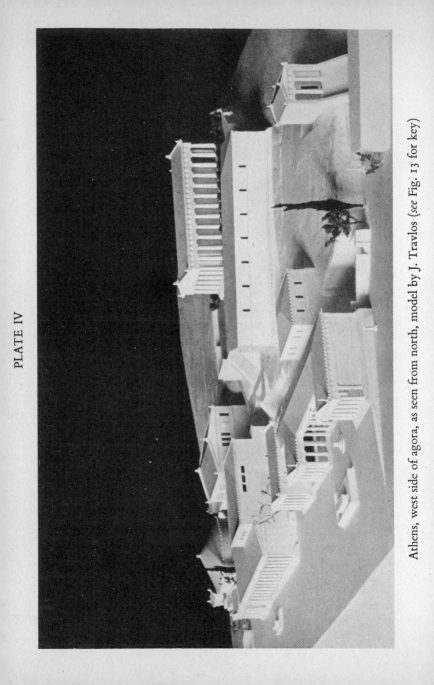

Athens, west side of agora, as seen from north, model by J. Travlos (*see* Fig. 13 for key)

PLATE V

Miletus, harbour and north agora, model by H. Schleif, in the Pergamon Museum, Berlin

In the background, beyond the stoas of the north agora, can be seen (*left to right*) the nymphaeum, the gateway of the south agora, and the
upper part of the council house

PLATE VI

Olympia, model by H. Schleif, in the Olympia Museum, as from north-east

PLATE VII

(a) Delphi, sanctuary of Apollo, model by H. Schleif (by courtesy of the Metropolitan Museum of Art, New York)

(b) Athens, Acropolis, model by G. P. Stevens, in the Toronto Museum

PLATE VIII

(a) Unfinished temple at Segesta (Sicily) (*photo*, Marburg Seminar)

The temple was built about 430 B.C. The unfinished state of the columns, still without fluting, emphasizes the simple grandeur of the Doric order. The inner structure has been removed.

(b) Ionic temple of Artemis at Ephesus, as rebuilt in fourth century B.C. (restoration, Krischen, Pl. 36)

The sculptured column-drums are a very rare feature. The barbaric cult-image can be seen through the door

PLATE IX

Stoa of Athenians, Delphi (*photo*, Hellenic Society)

PLATE X

Megalopolis, theatre and thersilion (*photo*, German Archaeological Institute).

Little more than the foundations of the thersilion survive; the bases of the interior columns stand in rows

PLATE XI

View to east from Delphi, with gymnasium (*photo*, Hellenic Society)

The circular bath can be clearly seen ; beyond it is the palaestra, and, on the higher terrace above, the colonnade of the covered running track

PLATE XII

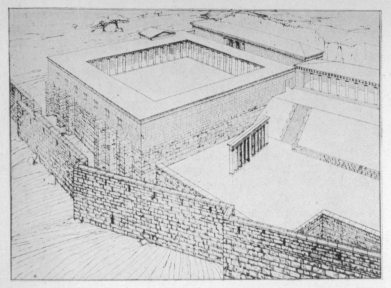

(a) Priene, lower gymnasium, stadium and city-wall
(restoration, M. Schede, *Priene*, Abb. 99)

(b) Stadium attached to shrine of Asclepius at Epidaurus
(*photo*, by D. M. Jones)

In its present state this stadium gives a good idea of the simpler type of stadium or of the primitive *dromos* type of gymnasium. It was never fully provided with stone seating

PLATE XIII

(a) Athens, primitive theatre and temple of Dionysus (restoration, Fiechter, *Dionysos-Theater*, iii, Abb. 29)

(b) Theatre attached to shrine of Asclepius, Epidaurus
(*photo*, German Archaeological Institute)

In the middle distance, *right*, are the remains of the *Katagogion*, a hostel for visitors, built round four courts ; the stadium stretches to the *left*, below the modern road

PLATE XIV

(a) Priene, street leading from agora (restoration, Krischen,
Pl. 22)

In foreground, north end of west stoa of agora, in background, houses

(b) House-model from Perachora (*photo*, Hellenic Society)

Parts of columns and roof are restored with the help of other models

PLATE XV

(a) 'Villa of Good Fortune', Olynthus (restoration, *Olynthus*, viii, frontispiece)

(b) Courtyard of house, Priene (restoration, Krischen, Pl. 18)

Note the handsome porch of the main room on the north, and the lower colonnade on the east, which leads from the main entrance

PLATE XVI

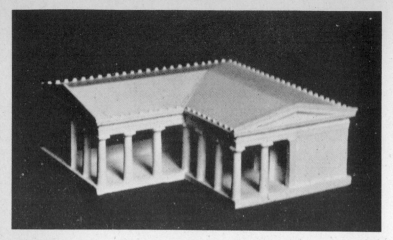

(a) South-west fountain-house at Athens, model by J. Travlos and C. Mammelis (*photo*, by Alison Frantz). See Ch. VIII supplementary n. 1.

(b) Fountain-house at Ialysos, Rhodes (*photo*, by T. J. Dunbabin)

a reasonable inference. The new late fifth-century building, which stood a little to the west, was slightly smaller (22·5 m. by 17·5 m.). The main indication of its interior arrangement is that the dressed bedrock slopes gently down from north, west and south as a theatre slopes down to its orchestra. Passages were left between the east wall and the retaining walls of the wings of the auditorium. Two columns stood in the line of these retaining walls and two others towards the back of the auditorium. The entrances were at the south-east and north-east corners and possibly also in the middle of the east side. Thus the general scheme is fairly well established, but the original nature of the seating is quite conjectural,[24] and the reconstruction with curved marble benches in tiers cannot be earlier than Hellenistic times, though there must have been some simple theatral arrangement with wooden seats earlier. As in most council-houses of this type, there is no trace of a raised platform for the speakers ; they must simply have taken their stand in the ' orchestra ', unless they had a wooden bema which has left no trace, or simply rose in their places.

Curiously, the new Council-House was rather small for the 500 it was supposed to contain ; McDonald aptly compares the House of Commons. It had something in the nature of a public gallery, but we do not know how this was contrived. It contained statues, paintings, an altar of Zeus and Athena and numerous slabs on which decrees were inscribed.

The unobtrusive position of this most important public building is surprising to us, tucked away as it was first behind the old Council-House and then behind the enlarged Hellenistic Metroön. Its east side, which should normally have been the front, could hardly receive monumental treatment ; but on the south there was a small open court, and on this side a columnar façade was added early in the third century, possibly at the same time as the somewhat awkwardly placed pro-pylon which led to the Council-House through a passage from the east. Thus, though the Athenian Council-House was well planned *inside* and foreshadowed the grander Milesian, its position and relation to neighbour-ing public buildings were not so well managed ; it did not take the prominent place one would expect in the architecture of the agora, and was a little awkward of access. The same may, in fact, be said of the treatment of official buildings as of shrines in the older cities. There was little attempt to correlate groups of buildings closely, still less to lead up to and set off an important building by means of subsidiary structures formally arranged. A contrast may be drawn between the Council-House of Athens and the Assembly-Hall of Priene, which though hemmed in closely on all sides so that it could not receive a monumental front of its own, was effect-ively and conveniently knit into the plan of the city and the agora, and shared the Sacred Stoa as a façade (fig. 18) ; still greater is the contrast between the hand-some peristyle and entrance gateway of the Council-House at Miletus, and the small unadorned courtyard and awkwardly placed *propylon* at Athens.[25] Yet even in Hippodamian cities the more elaborate and artificial forms of axial and symmetrical planning are absent.

The Assembly-Hall of Priene (built about 200 B.C.) had seats for six or seven hundred. The exterior was unpretentious, but the interior was very well designed

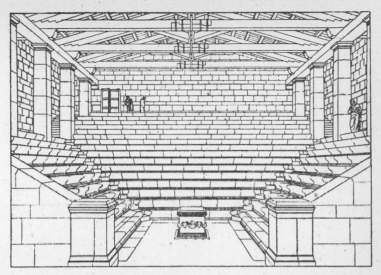

FIG. 37. Council-House, Priene (restoration, Krischen, Pl. 26)

and handsome. From a flat square, on which stood an altar, sixteen rows of stone seats rose to the north and ten to the east and west, advantage being taken of the natural slope. Fourteen pillars on the topmost tier helped to support the wooden roof, but the span was considerable even so (14·5 m.). Behind the pillars ran a gangway. Between the south wall and the retaining walls of the seating were passages like the *parodoi* of a theatre, and the south wall itself was broken by two doors and a broad rectangular niche with seats which were no doubt intended for officials.

The Council-House of Miletus was built 175–164 B.C. and was dedicated to Apollo, Hestia and Demos (the People). The seating formed rather more than a semicircle, just as in a theatre. The advantage of the semicircular form over the rectangular was that seeing

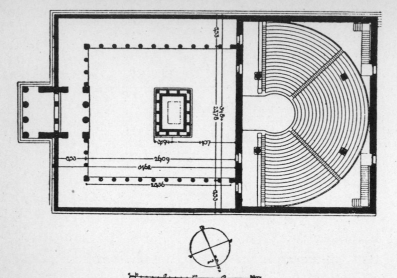

FIG. 38. Council-House, Miletus (*Milet*, i. 2, Abb. 53)

and hearing were easier ; its disadvantage that it did not fit so well into a rectangular building and left awkward corners. At Miletus some use was made of the corners by introducing stairways from the two back doors ; one wonders also whether the platforms which occupied the rest of the space were public galleries, and whether this was so at Athens too. Four interior supports were unobtrusively placed as in the new Council-House at Athens. This arrangement and the ⊓ form of Priene are the main methods of roof-support, and Athens provides forerunners for both. The chamber measured about 22 m. by 33 m., and would seat quite 1200 people. The exterior was more ornate than in most predecessors. The walls were decorated in their upper half with engaged half-columns ; and there were pediments at the north and south ends. Extending eastwards from the front

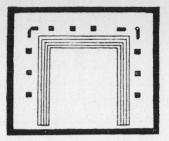

Fig. 39.   Council-House, Notium (*Ath. Mit.* xi, p. 422)

was a colonnaded court, entered by a propylon and containing an ornate hero-shrine. The Council-House of Miletus was the most stately of its kind, and by reason of the size of the chamber the most remarkable in construction. Its strict symmetry about an axis running through propylon, tomb and auditorium foreshadow the more complex and grandiose symmetrical schemes which became common in later architecture.

One or two other specimens may be mentioned. Sicyon had a large council-house, built about 300 B.C. ; its dimensions were 40·5 m. by 39·6 m.,²⁶ and it had sixteen interior supports in four rows ; but the auditorium occupied only a limited part of this large hall. Notium, near Colophon, had a simple version of the Priene type, built in the third or second century. The square building at the east end of the agora at Assos (fig. 20), with four interior supports and, on the west, six doors separated by five columns, was probably a council-house, built early in the second century. McDonald lists numerous other possible examples, but they add little ; their plans, and even their identification, are often too uncertain to give much value to the evidence they provide.

The final form of the bouleuterion, a small rectangular or semicircular theatre set within four walls and roofed over, with interior supports in one of the two forms ⌐ or ∶∶, may be considered another ingenious creation of the Greek architects, developed from simple traditional elements to satisfy practical requirements. Again there is no need to talk about external models and foreign influence. Leroux thinks [27] the arrangement of the columns in the Priene form an adaptation of an Egyptian type ; but it is inevitably suggested by the rectangular arrangement of the seating, which is itself suggested by the external form of the hall.

In Roman times many small covered theatres were built for musical performances and recitations ; they were called Odeion or Odeum, though the name and the function belonged to other types too, including a rectangular building with numerous internal columns, erected at Athens in the time of Pericles. The council-house too could obviously be used for such performances ; we hear of musical recitals in the Council-House at Teos and declamations at Elis and Smyrna, and in several council-houses, including the Milesian, a stage was added at a late phase.[28]

The prytaneion is hardly a distinct architectural type, since it is nothing more than a kind of house, but functionally it is very interesting and important. Its essential feature was the common hearth, symbol of the communal life of the city, on which a perpetual fire was maintained and to which the cult of Hestia, goddess of the hearth, was attached. The building also contained a dining-room in which meals were given to officials, foreign ambassadors and other distinguished visitors, and citizens who had brought benefits or glory to their country, for example, by a successful embassy or a victory in a race at Olympia. The prytaneion was the successor of the king's house in function. The word ' prytanis ' primarily means ' chief ', though at Athens it was appropriated for the select committee of Council. The State, even when it was no longer embodied in one man, needed a domestic centre, a house which belonged to the whole community rather than an individual citizen, where it could offer hospitality. *Hôtel-de-Ville* is a better equivalent for ' prytaneion ' than the usual English translation ' Town-Hall '.

In many cities the prytaneion must have been of great antiquity. One might expect the survival of archaic forms, as in the Council-House at Olympia, but there is little evidence for this. It has been suggested [29] that the prytaneion was normally round, like Italian temples of Vesta, whose cult was analogous to that of Hestia, and that it retained the form of the primitive circular hut. Some prytaneia may have been circular, for all we know, but the surviving examples are far from proving that this was usual. The Tholos at Athens was indeed round, but its archaic predecessor was quite different.

Olympia again provides an interesting specimen. The Prytaneion there was one of the oldest buildings on the site. In its classical form, which was later much complicated by reconstructions, a vestibule on the south led into a square room which probably contained the hearth. On either side of this was a small courtyard, and along the outer side of each ran a colonnade. The western colonnade was probably one of the dining-halls,

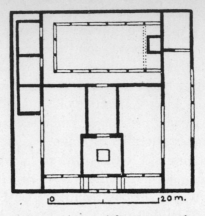

FIG. 40. Prytaneion, Olympia (after E. N. Gardiner, *Olympia*, fig. 114 ; Curtius and Adler, *Olympia*, i. 44)

and the small rooms at the north end seem to have been kitchens. From the square room a narrower chamber led to a larger court at the back. The whole building formed a square.

The Prytaneion of Athens is problematical. Pausanias saw it north of the Acropolis and south-east of the Agora (i. 18. 3), but it is not certain that it was always there.[30] Slight remains have been found which *may* belong to it, but the identification is not proved. Besides the Prytaneion proper the Athenians had a sort of duplicate in the *Tholos*, also called *Skias*, where the *prytaneis* (presidents or committee of council) ate and offered sacrifice, and where official weights and measures were kept, some of which have been found. The Tholos in its original fifth-century form was a circular building about 18 m. in diameter, with six interior columns. The entrance was on the east and was given a columnar porch in late Hellenistic times ; on the north was an

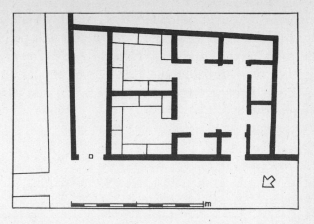

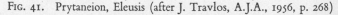

FIG. 41. Prytaneion, Eleusis (after J. Travlos, A.J.A., 1956, p. 268)

annexe which no doubt contained the kitchen. The Tholos was conveniently near the Council-House, unlike the Prytaneion. The latter, in addition to its normal functions, was used by certain magistrates and was the scene of an extraordinary primitive court of law in which inanimate objects were tried for murder, and contained a further copy of the laws of Solon and a number of honorary statues.

The indistinctness of the type makes identification difficult where there is no clear topographical or inscriptional evidence. But where a house-like building, distinguished perhaps by a monumental entrance, is found attached to the agora among other public buildings it may be tentatively labelled prytaneion. Ancient tradition may have fixed the site elsewhere in some old towns, but the choice of a site near the agora was normal, and here the prytaneion may be found in Hippodamian cities. We have met an example at Miletus. At Priene the identification is practically certain ; the peristyle with rooms on three sides, adjoining the Assembly-Hall, can hardly have been anything else ; the hearth was perhaps in the room at the south-east corner. At Magnesia the Prytaneion was probably the building of similar form and position, but more spacious, at the south-west corner of the agora.[31]

VI

GYMNASIUM,[1] STADIUM
AND THEATRE

GYMNASION means a place where people strip for exercise. Gymnastics played a great part in Greek life ; *gymnastike* was complementary to *mousike* (music and literature) in the normal scheme of education. Suitable areas had to be set aside where boys and young men could run, ride, box, wrestle, throw the discus or play ball games. The gymnasium is to be thought of primarily as an extensive athletic ground rather than a closely knit architectural unit. It was a centre for mental as well as physical training, and inevitably became a centre of general social life, like the agora and the stoas. In time appropriate buildings were put up in and around the athletic ground — stoas, baths, dressing-rooms, storerooms, class- and lecture-rooms and so forth. The *palaestra* or wrestling-ground was, strictly speaking, part of the gymnasium, though it could also exist in its own right. But it was an important part ; and when athletic buildings attained a well-developed architectural form, the most characteristic part. So it is not surprising that the proper distinction between the two words is not maintained and they tend to become interchangeable.[2] The normal type of athletic building which was finally evolved consisted of a colonnaded court surrounded by various rooms ; and it is sometimes called gymnasium, sometimes palaestra, though such buildings could hardly be in themselves all that the old extensive gymnasia were.

It has already been pointed out that the gymnasium was a place of spiritual as well as physical education. This needs further emphasis and explanation before we consider the nature of the gymnasium and its place in the city. The name 'gymnasium', like 'palaestra', refers to physical training ; this is not surprising ; the needs of athletic and military exercise would determine in the first place where the gymnasia should be situated and what form they should take ; and in the education of early times there would be an emphasis — by no means lost even later — on the production of good soldiers. But the Hellenic ideal was a perfect harmony between physical and intellectual education ; neither should be allowed to become a mere adjunct of the other ; they should not even proceed separately side by side ; they should be closely interwoven and both contribute to the moulding of the whole man. This was an ideal which could hardly be consistently realized, but it had a profound effect on educational practice, and the union between *gymnastike* and *mousike* and even *philosophia* was reflected in the life of the gymnasium and in its arrangement and architectural form.

Schools, which were numerous in the large cities, were mainly private institutions till late, and architecturally may be classed with houses, save that some had a palaestra of their own (others had to hire a palaestra or use the public gymnasia). But in the Greek ideal, 'schooling' was only a part of *paideia*, which included all formative influences on the body and mind. Parents of course were 'teachers', but so also were political leaders, and the poets — especially in the theatre — and many others ; and nowhere had these broad educative influences better opportunities of taking effect than in the public gymnasia. Boys and men of all sorts and ages frequented them, for exercise, for strenuous athletic training, for instruction and for general recreation.

Every Greek town had its gymnasium ; it was one of those elements like the agora without which the polis was incomplete, as Pausanias well knew (x. 4. 1). Large cities had two or more gymnasia, besides additional palaestrae. Athens, besides her three ancient and renowned gymnasia, acquired four or five others later. Various officials were appointed to supervise the activities of the gymnasia, though the latter were not too formally and elaborately organized in the greatest days ; this is not the place to go into details of organization or the scheme of Greek education and its different stages, but one may note that the special care given to them shows the importance of the gymnasia in the life of the city.

It may be that at an early phase the agora included among its many functions that of ' village green ', where boys and young men could practise for and hold athletic contests and play games, and older people could gather to watch them. It is a reasonable assumption and there is some slight evidence associating the agora with athletics, as we shall see in dealing with the stadium. But even so, the agora would become less and less suitable as time went on, and from an early date this function belonged to the gymnasia. Various factors helped to decide where these should grow. Religious associations were strong and the early gymnasia were invariably attached to the shrine of some appropriate deity or some local hero.

Hermes and Heracles in particular were the gods of the gymnasium, but the cults showed great variety. Plutarch gives an interesting, comparatively late historical example (*Timoleon* 39. 5): the city of Syracuse gave its liberator Timoleon a grave and hero-shrine in the agora, with games in his honour; around this later grew a handsome gymnasium, with stoas, gardens and an odeum. The deity or hero frequently gave his name to the gymnasium. Apart from considerations of cult, a secluded spot was preferable, where training could go on in quiet, pleasant and healthy surroundings. Shady trees were desirable and a good supply of water was essential; a natural spring near at hand was an advantage; otherwise water would have to be brought by conduits. The gymnasium was often closely associated with the stadium, in which case its position was decided by the factors governing the choice of a site for the stadium. In these various circumstances gymnasia are naturally found in very different sites in different cities. The older gymnasia showed a preference for the edge of the city or the suburbs, where they could spread themselves on spacious park-like lines. But we find old gymnasia within the walls too, and even in the heart of the city (Sicyon, Elis). In later times this was more frequently so (*e.g.* Megalopolis, the gymnasium of Ptolemy at Athens).[3] When the peristyle type of gymnasium or palaestra had been evolved, a place for it could be found more naturally in the architecture of the inner city. In towns with chess-board streets it could occupy a block or several blocks. In fact, rectangular street-planning may have helped to suggest and develop a compact rectangular form for the gymnasium and for other buildings too. There was still no normal place for the gymnasium in the scheme ; it might be near the agora, as at Miletus, or on the extreme edge ; at Priene the lower gymnasium was on the southern edge and somewhat detached, though still conforming to the general orientation ; the upper was embedded in the street system and displaced one house-block. The gymnasium of Nicaea, as described by Strabo (xii. 565), must have been exceptional ; from it one could look out along the streets and see the four main gates of the city ; a gymnasium would not normally have such a key position in the exact centre.

About the form of the earliest gymnasia we know little. But even the absence of evidence is informative ; architecturally there can be little to know. Fougères [4] very reasonably saw four periods in the history of the gymnasium ; in the first there was nothing more than a *dromos*, a running-course or sports ground ; the second is the archaic period, for which Athens will provide examples ; the third is the fourth century and Hellenistic age ; the fourth the Roman period, which is outside our present range. A highly developed architectural form for the gymnasium is comparatively late.

We have a good deal of general information about the ancient gymnasia of Athens — the Academy, the Lyceum and Cynosarges. The Academy was the most famous of all gymnasia. It lay about three-quarters of a mile outside the north-western gates of the city. The name was derived from an obscure old hero, Academus, or rather, originally, Hecademus, whose worship was associated with that of Prometheus and Hephaestus. Athena too was worshipped there, and her shrine contained twelve sacred olives ; Zeus had an altar, and so had Hermes and Heracles. The gymnasium goes back at least to the days of the tyrants in the sixth century ; we hear of a wall built by Hipparchus. Under Cimon in the fifth century it became a kind of public park ; Cimon improved the water supply and planted trees of various kinds (Plutarch, *Cimon* 13). Aristophanes in the *Clouds* (1005 ff.) gives a delightful picture of the Academy with its trees :

> But you will below to the Academe go, and under the olives contend
> With your chaplet of reed, in a contest of speed with some excellent rival and friend :
> All fragrant with woodbine and peaceful content, and the leaf which the lime-blossoms fling,
> When the plane whispers love to the elm in the grove in the beautiful season of spring.[5]

The picture may probably be taken as true in general of the old suburban gymnasia.

The Lyceum and Cynosarges must have been similar. The Lyceum was a shrine of Apollo in the eastern suburbs, and must have been very extensive since it was used for cavalry manœuvres — as was the Academy also — and for mustering troops. It too was planted with trees. Cynosarges — the name was a mystery even to the ancients — was to the south of the city, beyond the river Ilissus. Heracles was the chief deity of the place, but some of his friends and relations had altars too — Alcmene, Iolaus and Hebe. Thus Athens was almost ringed with these pleasant spots, in which shrine, gymnasium and park were combined, and athletic, social and intellectual life blossomed freely. The layout of such old gymnasia must have been informal and varied. Besides the trees and open spaces there would be shrines (normally of a simple character, not great temples), altars, enclosing walls, running-tracks and other simple facilities for games and practice, and stoas ; there would be statues, becoming more and more thick upon the ground, of gods, heroes and men, including founders, benefactors and successful athletes. In the fourth century each of the three suburban gymnasia of Athens became the seat of a philosophical school. Informal political and ethical discussions had been and still were frequent among *habitués* and visitors ; Socrates frequented the Lyceum and other gymnasia. But the tendency was for groups to crystallize as schools around particular teachers in particular places. Plato established his school, not indeed in the old gymnasium itself, but in a piece of property adjacent to the shrine. This institution, the mother of all universities, at first an appendage of the Academy, presently took the name to itself. In Cynosarges Antisthenes and the Cynics found a home. The school of Aristotle, the Peripatetics, identified itself with the Lyceum. Very like Plato, Theophrastus had a garden near the gymnasium, with a stoa and a shrine of the Muses ; this he left by will for the use of the school. Because of their importance in Athenian life in general, but more particularly because of their association with the philosophical schools, the gymnasia have a hardly less intense significance for the history of humanity than the acropolis or the agora. One would like to know much more of them. Certain scanty remains associated doubtfully with Cynosarges tell us little, even if their identification were reliable. A few years before the War excavations by Greek archaeologists identified the exact site of the Academy, and interesting remains of an enclosure, a shrine, a palaestra and other structures were found ; but the topography of the site is not yet clear.

No doubt there was something unique about Athens in the number and spirit of her gymnasia. One may compare and contrast the *platanistas* at Sparta, surrounded by a moat with two bridges and ringed with plane trees (Pausanias iii. 14. 8). Here, as part of the training prescribed by Lycurgus, the young Spartans fought one another ferociously and hurled one another into the water. Near by was the dromos or running-track, with two gymnasia, and shrines of heroes and deities ; the Dioscuri (' Sons of Zeus ', Castor and Pollux) were worshipped here under the title Apheterii or Starters. All this was in the western part of the city.

Pausanias' description of Elis gives an interesting picture of an old gymnasium to which had been added buildings of the new type. Pausanias says (vi. 23. 1) that the old gymnasium, in which the athletes trained before going on to Olympia, was one of the most noteworthy things in Elis. It had plane trees growing between the running-tracks within a wall ; there was a place where the stewards matched the competitors in wrestling ; there were altars of Heracles and other deities, including Love and Love Returned (Anteros ; Love also had an altar and statue in the Academy), and a cenotaph of Achilles. There was also another ' gymnasium-enclosure ', called Square because of its shape, and used for wrestling ; clearly this was what in more precise terms would be called a palaestra. Yet another ' gymnasium-enclosure ', containing palaestrae, was reserved for the youths, and also found room for the Council-House, where exhibitions of extempore speeches and recitations were held. Though so extensive, the Elean gymnasium was inside the city, just west of the agora.

Of gymnasia which consist of a number of miscellaneous elements not closely knit into a compact architectural unit, the Delphian provides the most plentiful archaeological evidence. The great national shrines, since they were centres for important athletic festivals, naturally had their own gymnasia and palaestrae, though the use of these would be concentrated in festival times and they would not be places of constant gymnastic and social resort. The Gymnasium of Delphi was magnificently situated, east of the shrine of Apollo, high above the valley of the Pleistus and beneath the towering cliffs of Parnassus (Pl. XI). Some ingenuity was needed to adapt such a site to the needs of a gymnasium, and the slope was reduced to two terraces. On these were disposed running-tracks, colonnades, an irregular enclosure with wash-basins and a circular plunge-bath, and a square palaestra and a number of subsidiary rooms. The existing remains are mainly of the fourth century, but the gymnasium was no doubt a good deal older. Pausanias says (x. 8. 8) that there was formerly a wild wood on the site, and there were no doubt trees in the gymnasium too.

In the fourth century, and still more in the Hellenistic age, a more sophisticated and less informal type of building came into use for gymnastic and general training. It could still be part of a more extensive conglomeration, as was the palaestra at Delphi, but it could also be a self-contained establishment and a complete architectural unit. It consisted of a square colonnaded court with various rooms along the sides, opening into the colonnades. The perfectly regular peristyle court was foreign to early Hellenic architecture, which preferred a certain informality and openness in the arrangement of colonnades and other elements. Leroux [6] indeed thinks that the peristyle was essentially Hellenistic, and denies the claims of peristyle gymnasia and other buildings of this form to earlier dates. But on the whole it seems probable that the peristyle, already tentatively employed, was coming into fuller use in the fourth century, for a variety of purposes. We have seen that the peristyle agora was a late un-Hellenic conception ; but the agora was more than a single building or than any ordinary collection of buildings, and its reduction

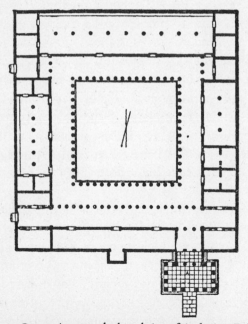

FIG. 42. Gymnasium attached to shrine of Asclepius, Epidaurus

to an enclosed colonnaded court meant a more funda-
mental change. Leroux thinks the peristyle gymnasium
merely a peristyle house with the court enlarged at the
expense of the rooms ; rather it is some of the elements
of the old loosely knit gymnasium reduced to a compact
and regular form under the influence of new architectural
ideas.

For a good example of the type we may go again
to an important shrine with a Pan-Hellenic clientele. In
the sanctuary of Asclepius near Epidaurus a large building
in the southern part of the area, immediately east of
the stadium, is reasonably identified with the gymnasium. It has been dated to the fourth century, though
Leroux denies this dating, stating dogmatically that it
is one of the most complete specimens of the Hellenistic
type. It is 75·57 m. long by 69·53 m. It had a magnificent colonnaded court ; on the north side the colonnade
was double. The surrounding rooms were of various
shapes and sizes. Some were large halls with interior
columns, others were quite small. At the west end of
the north side projected an impressive propylon, with
columns all round. There were also subsidiary entrances.
The interior of this building was completely remodelled
in Roman times as a small theatre or odeum. A little
to the north are remains of a building which is similar
but smaller and simpler ; this is tentatively identified as
a palaestra.

The palaestra at Olympia provides a very clear
example (see fig. 27). It was built towards the end of
the third century, but was still of a basically simple type.
It formed a precise square of 66 m. There was no
elaborate propylon as at Epidaurus but unobtrusive

entrances at the south corners. The plan speaks for itself, save that it does not indicate the identification and purpose of the different rooms. There is normally little in the remains to differentiate the rooms, since their arrangement and equipment are very simple. But we learn from Vitruvius (v. 11) and other sources the kind of thing to expect. There were rooms for undressing, for anointing with oil and powdering with dust, and for storing oil and equipment. The *ephebeion*, a sort of club-room and lecture-room, was one of the most important. There were bath-rooms, not elaborate and magnificent affairs as in Roman bathing establishments, but practical and austere.[7] The bath-room in the palaestra at Olympia, in the north-east corner, is identified by a large tank-like bath sunk in the floor ; but in others there were wash-basins or removable baths which, in some cases, must have vanished and left no trace. Small rooms near the entrance may have served the purpose of porter's lodge. In the large rooms looking out through open colonnades visitors may have sat and talked or rested, or watched the athletes practising wrestling, boxing, jumping and so forth in the courtyard. Amongst details of equipment and adornment one might mention statues, occasionally paintings, inscriptions of lists of pupils and athletic victors, and, in later times, libraries.

At Olympia there was also a building called ' gymnasium ', adjoining the palaestra on the north. The words which Pausanias uses in describing them (v. 15. 8, vi. 21. 2) seem to indicate that the palaestra may be considered a part or an adjunct of the gymnasium. The main part of the gymnasium, which was much more extensive than the palaestra, was given a monumental form rather later. The remains indicate a colonnade abutting on the north wall of the palaestra, a handsome entrance gateway at the south-east corner, and a great double colonnade along the eastern side, long enough to house a stade running-track, where athletes could practise under cover. Adjoining this, according to Pausanias, were the 'dwellings of the athletes'. The west side of the gymnasium has suffered badly from changes of course of the river Cladeus, and its arrangement is uncertain. The late date of these Olympic buildings is worth noting. In the great days of the festival the arrangements for practice, as for the actual contest, were presumably simple and austere.

It will be noticed that in the Palaestra of Olympia the rooms on the north side were deeper than the others, and in the middle was the largest and most important room of the whole building. This places a certain emphasis on the north side. The principle was carried a good deal further in a certain definitely Hellenistic type of gymnasium; this was rectangular, with an important building, higher than the rest, on one of the small sides; on this side there was also an Ionic colonnade, contrasting with the lower Doric columns of the other three sides (in the other type there were normally uniform columns all round). A good example is the gymnasium near the north agora of Miletus,[8] which was built in the second century B.C. This has a series of rooms behind an imposing Ionic colonnade on the north, simple Doric colonnades without rooms on the other sides, and an Ionic propylon in the middle of the south. It was naturally the north side which was given the greater height, so that the rooms would receive the winter sunshine. Von Gerkan (p. 106) finds that gymnasia of this type embody the same principle of architectural composition as the 'horseshoe' agora; but the complete enclosure, the emphasis on an axial line through the propylon and the main room on the opposite side, and the fact that the three uniform colonnades form two long and one short side, instead of two short and one long, make a considerable difference. A closer parallel is provided by such buildings as the Council-House of Miletus with its forecourt. The type also has a similarity to some Roman fora, and may have influenced them.

The lower gymnasium of Priene (second century) combines features of both types. The courtyard is square and the colonnade uniform all round. But the main rooms are concentrated on the north, including a handsome school- or lecture-room,[9] open on the front save for two columns, and this part was loftier than the rest of the building. The rooms did not open directly out of the north colonnade, but were separated from it by a narrow forecourt. The entrance, a very simple propylon, was not axially placed on the south side, but towards the north end of the west side. The north colonnade communicated conveniently with the adjoining stadium. In a gymnasium of the Priene design Greek architects had evolved a simple but very serviceable type of school-building, well designed both aesthetically and practically.

Into further developments of the gymnasium it is not necessary to enter here, except perhaps briefly by way of contrast. The great triple gymnasium of Pergamon was characteristically lavish in design; it occupied three terraces; on the highest was a great colonnaded court;

on the middle terrace was a long and comparatively narrow enclosure ; on the lowest a small irregular enclosure. In Roman times athletic establishments became infinitely more luxurious, though the old types too continued. In particular they were provided with elaborate hot baths. In fact these tended to become the dominant element, and at this stage gymnasium and thermae are sometimes almost synonymous terms.

Nothing could contrast more strongly with the original character of the Hellenic gymnasium, which was essentially practical and austere. Simple in its origins, it retained the quality of simplicity, not only in the old training grounds, but also in the more sophisticated types created in the fourth and succeeding centuries.

The stadium too [10] grew out of simple natural elements, and in the great days of Greek athletics and the Olympic festival was still rudimentary in form and architecturally unpretentious. One is apt to imagine that the magnificently reconstructed stadium of modern Athens, with its tiers of marble seats along the sides and curving round one end, and a monumental entrance at the other, gives a good idea of the appearance of a typical ancient stadium. In fact the Athenian stadium did not receive monumental treatment till the time of Lycurgus (fourth century B.C.), and the new building reproduces the form created by the lavish expenditure of money and marble by Herodes Atticus in the second century A.D. (Pausanias i. 19. 6). Such stadia did not exist in the fifth century B.C. and were probably in a minority to the end. Pausanias describes the stadium of the sanctuary of Asclepius near Epidaurus as 'consisting, like most Greek stadia, of a bank of earth' (ii. 27. 5).

The word *stadion* means a unit of distance, about 200 yds. with several local variations, a race run over this distance and the ground over which the race was run. The three meanings are closely bound up together, and it is difficult to show that any one is the primary sense; but certainly the use of the word for an artificially constructed race-course is secondary. The stade is about the limit of distance for which a man can run at full stretch. The stade race was of great antiquity; it was traditionally the oldest at Olympia where the greatest national games of Greece were held; to win it was the highest honour and the victors gave their names to the Olympiads or four-year periods of the games. The stadium was designed primarily for this race. A straight narrow course was laid out, about 200 yds. long, and the spectators lined this on either side. In longer races the competitors ran up and down the same course, doubling sharply round a turning-post or a series of turning-posts at the ends. The longer races were later accretions at Olympia, according to tradition, and no concession was made to them in the form of the course, though a circular or elliptical course, such as is used now, would have been more convenient. The stadium was sometimes used for boxing and wrestling too.

Thus the basic requirements were very limited; a flat or levelled piece of ground was needed, rather more than 200 yds. long, so as to leave a free space at each end, and wide enough for a dozen or a score of runners to line up abreast; actual widths vary considerably on either side of 100 ft. It was convenient for the spectators if the ground rose or was made to rise on both sides and perhaps at one or both ends. As so often the

Greeks looked to nature to provide a ready-made site with natural slopes. It is a far cry from the stadium even in its fully grown form to the Roman amphitheatre with its elaborate system of supporting vaults. When such substructures are found in a stadium it is a sure indication of late date. In earlier times, apart from the deficiency of constructional technique, greater economy was necessary. A long shallow trough between two low hills was an excellent site; best of all was a flattish valley running up into gently sloping ground, providing natural banking on both sides and one end, and leaving the other end open for the entrance. The Athenians found an almost ideal site to the south-east of their city, between two hills and with a slope at the further end too; the open end conveniently faced the city, where a bridge was built over the Ilissus stream (fig. 1). Failing these advantages, a natural embankment could at any rate be provided on one side, by placing the race-course at the foot of a slope, or on a terrace on a hillside; artificial banking would then be needed on the opposite side. In any case the slopes could be extended, completed and regularized artificially.

Obviously the choice of a site depended mainly on natural contours. The stadium had no normal place in the layout of the city, and no well-defined relation to other great buildings. Orientation varied greatly, with some preference for east to west. As we saw, the agora may have been the scene of games and sports in early times. It could hardly remain so in an architecturally sophisticated community, but we find one or two possible survivals which link the agora curiously with foot-racing. One of the streets which led from the Spartan agora was called Aphetais, or the Street of the Starting-Post, Pausanias says (iii. 12. 1), because, in a legendary race for the hand of Penelope, Odysseus and his unsuccessful rivals were said to have started their course along it. In the Agora of Corinth, on the east side, the excavators have found a starting-line (a row of stone slabs, with pairs of parallel grooves) for sixteen competitors ; its date is the third century B.C., but below it are remains of a fourth-century line of rather different form and orientation ; the races which took place here were probably of a ceremonial character.[11] But it would hardly be possible to accommodate a fully developed stadium in the built-up central area of a city. Sometimes the stadium was closely related to a gymnasium, as was natural ; in fact, the gymnasium being originally not simply a building but a quarter of the city devoted to athletics, the stadium might be thought of as a part or an appendage of it. On the other hand, some large gymnasia had full-size running-tracks of their own, sometimes under cover of a colonnade, for purposes of practice. The great size of the stadium meant that it was most frequently placed in the outskirts of the city, sometimes on the extreme edge but still within the circuit-walls, sometimes, where there was no suitable site within the city, well outside the walls. The arrangement at Aezani in Phrygia, by which the theatre and stadium are closely related, and the theatre encloses one end of the stadium, is late and anything but typical. The relation between the two great show-buildings of the Greek city is usually quite fortuitous.

In regularly planned towns with their rectangular streets the stadium was a rather unwieldy element to incorporate; it was inadvisable to let it cut awkwardly across a number of streets. Of course it could be detached completely from the main plan and placed right outside the city ; but by placing it on the edge and exercising a little ingenuity the Ionian architects were able to make it an effective unit in the Hippodamian plan. Miletus and Priene provide examples (see p. 164). In the former the great city wall made a convenient backing on the side on which artificial banking was necessary ; in the latter the wall was in the same position but there was no embankment on this side. Both had gymnasia adjacent.

The early development of the stadium can now be studied in the stadium of Olympia, the ' mother ' of Greek stadia, standing in the same relation to the rest as the theatre of Athens to other theatres. German archaeologists began a new investigation several years before the War,[12] and, although their work was cut short, they were able to define the stages by which the stadium grew. In the middle of the sixth century the slope of the hill north of the race-course was modified, and a low embankment was built on the south (it is possible that the western end, adjoining the shrine of Zeus, remained open until the fourth century). In the fifth century, perhaps about the time of the erection of the temple of Zeus, larger and more regular embankments were built. Another considerable enlargement took place in the fourth century, and a row of stone blocks was set along the foot of the banks. At the same time the track was remodelled, with lines of grooved stone slabs at either end to mark the starting- and finishing-points, and a water channel all round opening into basins. The provision of water was an important matter ; and so was drainage, since the situation of stadia on slopes or in gullies made them very liable to damage in times of heavy rain. The earlier arrangement of the track is obscure ; but it was no doubt very simple. Perhaps originally the start and finish were marked merely by posts and lines drawn on the ground. The sides of the stadium at Olympia, as in several others too, were not quite straight but bulged out a little in the middle to give the spectators a better view. The embankments were remodelled twice again in Roman times ; there was a tendency as time went on to make the slopes steeper. It will be noted that the great Olympic stadium remained to the end essentially a ' bank of earth ' as Pausanias says (vi. 20. 8), even when other stadia were being given tiers of seats of the same type as those used in the theatres. The same conservatism showed itself in the most venerable of stadia as in the most venerable of theatres, at Athens. The nearest approach at Olympia to the more developed form was that at a late stage the embankment or part of it was stepped, with light retaining walls to support the steps. On the south side a platform was provided for officials ; in its earliest extant form this belongs to the fourth-century stadium. The entrance, through which the judges and competitors trooped in from the Altis or sacred grove of Zeus, passing the bronze statues (Zanes in fig. 27) paid for by fines for breach of the rules, was at the north-west corner ; originally an open cutting, it was vaulted over in Roman times. Statues and altars completed the layout.

Though its later phases show remarkable conservatism, the Olympic stadium may probably be taken as

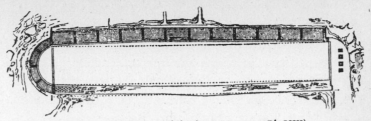

FIG. 43. Stadium, Delphi (*B.C.H.*, 1899, Pl. XIII)

typical in its early growth and its fifth- and even fourth-century form. The provision of stone or rock-cut seating on a large scale was probably exceptional before Hellenistic times ; when introduced it was modelled on the seating of the theatre, with stairways dividing it into blocks — wedges where there was a semicircular end — and a horizontal passage or *diazoma* half-way up in large stadia. Sometimes a wall or even a colonnade was built along the top.

The semicircular end (*sphendone*), so characteristic of the later form of stadium, probably only became customary in Hellenistic times. It is foreign to the original nature of the stadium, which was adapted to the needs of spectators standing along the sides of the stade course, and is due, at least partly, to the influence of the theatre. The sphendone could be used as a theatre for certain types of spectacle. It also helped to make the stadium approximate to the Roman amphitheatre, a very different type of building designed for a totally different type of performance. In fact at Athens and elsewhere arrangements were made for converting the stadium into a sort of amphitheatre for dangerous sports, with high barriers surrounding the track, now changed into an arena. Some late stadia have a sphendone at both ends.

The original simplicity of the stadium was masked still further in Roman times by the use of monumental columnar entrances and elaborate starting arrangements.[13] In later writers the words stadium and amphitheatre are sometimes used with little distinction, along with hippodrome, which originally meant a large course like a magnified stadium for horse- and chariot-races.

The history of the Greek theatre [14] is a vast and complicated subject. The literary and archaeological evidence is peculiarly difficult to handle, and has produced a mass of controversial literature. For the present purpose, which is to define the place of the theatre in the general architectural framework of the city, giving only the essentials of its form, it will not be necessary to become very deeply involved in these controversies or to attempt to solve these problems. They concern most particularly the ' stage-building ' (skene) which was originally the least essential part of the whole and remained for some time loosely attached to the rest, not reaching full development till Hellenistic times.

We now use the word ' stage ' in a general way meaning ' theatre ', ' drama ' ; to use it similarly of the classical Greek theatre involves an anachronism, or at least an incorrect emphasis. The heart of the Greek theatre was the orchestra, a ' dancing-place ' consisting of a flat piece of hard earth, usually though not necessarily approximating to a circle. This must be regarded as the nucleus, whether we think of the historical growth of the theatre or its developed form. Here the ancient rites, songs and dances, out of which the drama grew, could be performed. These ritual performances provided a spectacle for those not directly participating ;

so, secondly, a convenient place had to be found for the spectators, a *theatron* or 'place for seeing'. This was best provided by a slope rising above the flat orchestra, or best of all enclosing it on three sides in a hollow, though there is also some evidence for wooden stands, which had an inconvenient habit of collapsing, in early times. The name theatron came to be applied to the whole because the auditorium was the overwhelmingly dominant element. The orchestra — although it remained the focal point and the whole great theatron converged on it — was architecturally almost non-existent. Thirdly, as the drama developed, some further provision had to be made for the performers. The original simplicity of this element is shown by its name skene (tent, booth, hut). It furnished a background for the performance, and in time put forth a stage and encroached on the function and space of the orchestra; but originally, and in the great days of Attic drama, it was simple, subordinate and, until late in the fifth century, not permanent.

It has been necessary to take a preliminary glimpse at the form of the theatre before considering its place in the city, because the latter depends directly on the former. Equally with the stadium, and more so than most buildings, the theatre had its site determined by natural contours. Other factors counted too. A theatre designed to accommodate the populace of a large town needed plenty of space ; again, as the drama was associated with the worship of Dionysus, the theatre was sometimes associated with an ancient shrine of this god.

The Greeks liked to take the main structure of their theatres ready made from nature. The cost of material and labour was a restraining factor as always in the Greek cities before they acquired wealthy foreign patrons; and they had not at their command the technique of building arches and vaults which enabled architects in Roman times to erect imposing theatres and amphitheatres from ground level. The elementary needs of a theatre site were a flattish place for an orchestra and a slope rising from it for an auditorium; this would best be found at the foot of a hill which was not too steep and rocky; or, if the theatre were laid out higher up the hillside, a flat orchestra could be made by terracing. Few Greek cities were built upon entirely level ground and most possessed a suitable if not an ideal site. Only in exceptional cases do we find a theatre built up from level ground, as at Mantinea, or excavated in the middle and banked up round the circumference, as in a reconstruction at Eretria. On a level site a position could be chosen at will and the theatre made to conform with some regularly planned scheme. But the normal method of building on whatever happened to be the most convenient hillside meant that the theatre had no recognized place; and in fact it is found in many different parts of the city and suburbs.

That is not to say that theatres were not effectively and often magnificently sited in relation to the city as a whole, and their surroundings both natural and artificial. Set on a dominant hillside, the theatre must often have been one of the outstanding monuments of the town; and, on the other hand, the upper tiers often command particularly fine views over city, valley and sea.

A few tentative generalizations can be made about

the position of the theatre. The auditoria face almost all points of the compass, but there is naturally some preference for a southern outlook. The obvious slope on which to build was that of the acropolis, and here the theatre is often found, enhancing the architectural magnificence of the acropolis and itself gaining something from its setting. A certain relation can be detected between the theatre and the agora, though the connection in time wore thin and the theatre achieved independence. We can well imagine that the early agora was the scene of some of the performances out of which the drama grew, and the site of a rudimentary theatre. In the agora at Athens was a place called the orchestra, where in early times dances and dramatic performances were given, and probably temporary wooden seating was erected for the spectators. Bulle [15] sees a simple village agora in the 'theatres' of certain Attic demes, such as Rhamnus, where, at the foot of a slope below the acropolis wall, there was a row of stone seats for the dignitaries, facing a large flat terrace ; the remains are not very early, but may still give us some idea what a primitive agora combined with theatre was like. Where the agora was close under the acropolis, the slope of the latter immediately above was an obviously convenient and impressive site. In a fair number of towns the theatre even in its fully developed form was in the central area and in the neighbourhood of the agora. It must not be forgotten that in many cities it was the place of general assembly. But normally it would be difficult to accommodate a large theatre in the agora itself or the buildings immediately around it, though a place might be found for an odeum — a smaller building in the form of a roofed hall, possibly with theatre-like seating, used for musical contests and other purposes. Mantinea is exceptional in having a theatre (third century) which is closely knit into the architectural scheme of the agora, forming its western end; this theatre was no doubt used as an assembly-place. In this connection one may mention the position of the huge theatre of Megalopolis; the Agora of Megalopolis was on the north bank of the river Helisson, but the Thersilion, the great assembly-hall of the Arcadian league, was on the other bank immediately opposite; the theatre was built, in the middle of the fourth century, immediately to the south, with its auditorium facing the Thersilion (see p. 124 and Pl. X); the south porch of the latter took the place of stage-buildings.[16]

In Hippodamian towns the theatre required careful treatment and presented something of a problem; it did not fit so simply and obviously into the chess-board plan as the stoas of the agora, and the shrines and gymnasia, which occupied a block or several blocks conveniently. Even in these towns it had no normal and recognized place and was dealt with in a variety of ways. The difficulty was comparable to that of the architects who attempted to design a council-house by placing semicircular seating in a rectangular building, but it involved other problems, too, because of the size of a fully developed theatre and the need for a suitable sloping site. Sometimes it was possible to make the theatre conform to the street plan and even to fit it closely into the Hippodamian system; sometimes it was separately treated and had its own orientation. One may contrast Miletus and Priene. At Miletus, while the stadium was cunningly worked into the general plan, in a western extension of the agora area, the theatre on the other side of a bay of the sea was more detached and differently orientated. At Priene the stadium was placed obliquely at the lower edge of the town and was balanced by the theatre at the top, and the theatre conformed to the house-blocks. In both cases the theatre was on the edge of the built-up area. At Cnidos too (see von Gerkan, Abb. 10) the theatre was well placed in a slope at the top of the town, orientated with the house-blocks but detached from them. There are signs of thoughtful planning, but no uniformity of method.

To return to the form of the theatre — Miss Bieber aptly sums up its development : [17] ' the orchestra was created in the archaic age, the theatron in the classical age, when it achieved its final perfection. The scene building, on the other hand, found its typical form only in the late classical period. . . . Its development belongs to the Hellenistic period.' She adds, ' The most important thing to bear in mind is that in the classical age there was no such thing as a raised stage'. This last statement is possibly true ; but it can probably never be finally proved, and to be safer one might be less dogmatic and say that there was no arrangement which segregated the actors from the orchestra and the chorus and put them on a markedly different plane ; the area used for the performance was essentially one.

The orchestra remained an expanse of hard earth throughout. Ornamental paving — not so comfortable to dance on — was not introduced till Roman times. Originally the orchestra was not necessarily circular, and its circle was not always fully defined even in a well-developed theatre, though room was left for the possible completion of the circumference until the *proskenion* and finally the stage encroached. The centre might be marked by a base for an altar, and the circumference or the part of it adjoining the auditorium by a line of slabs and possibly a water channel.

The auditorium was ultimately made rather more than a semicircle,[18] by hollowing out the slope in the middle and banking it up at the ends; the embankment needed strong retaining walls at the back and at the ends above the parodoi or passages leading into the orchestra on either side. The curve of the auditorium was made to open out slightly at the ends; that is, the end sections of the seating were laid out on a slightly longer radius than the middle; this improved the view of the spectators in these parts, and facilitated the filling and emptying of the theatre. A horizontal passage (diazoma), or more rarely two, divided the seating into ranges, and radiating stairways, naturally more numerous in the upper part, into wedges. Sometimes part of the seating, especially at the top of the theatre, was cut in the native rock.[19] The seats were simple stone slabs, except perhaps for a few more ornamental and comfortable seats for officials and priests at the front; usually each tier overlapped the one below a little; their lowness and hardness imply that the spectators would bring cushions. These auditoria are hardly surpassed for architectural beauty; and in the absence of ornament the effect is obtained solely by the severe grace and harmony of the whole design.

The skene cannot be summed up so easily. While it contributes less to the architectural character of the classical Greek theatre than the auditorium, it is a much more complex subject. Some of the problems it raises will be touched upon later ; for the moment it may be noted that in the true Greek theatre the stage-building and auditorium remained separate, facing one another across the orchestra. The auditorium came to an abrupt end in the retaining walls. Light ornamental gateways thrown across the parodoi, as at Epidaurus, can hardly be said to unite the two elements in anything but a superficial way. It was left to Roman architects to link up the stage-building solidly with the ends of the auditorium so as to produce a single structure, in the process reducing the auditorium and the orchestra, which now served as part of the auditorium, to a semicircle. The Roman form was more complete and had a closer unity, but was hardly more beautiful in its lines and proportions. And if the Greek theatre did not attain formal architectural unity, it had a unity of spirit impossible in most later theatres. There was no impassable dividing-line such as is formed by the edge of a high stage, on which the whole action of the play takes place. The orchestra was a link between the skene and the auditorium, holding them together rather than keeping them apart. This is most obvious in comedy, where actors and chorus often approach the audience across the orchestra and address them or individual spectators directly ; but in tragedy too, in a more subtle way, the audience could feel themselves at one with the performers in the celebration of the dramatic ritual, as they were when they clustered on the hillside above and around the primitive orchestra.

The early development of the theatre can be seen best, though even so not very clearly, in the Dionysus theatre at Athens, the prototype of Greek theatres. This has been studied again very carefully by archaeologists in recent years ; and though the evidence is often very scanty, though many points are disputed and must remain conjectural, and absolute dating is usually impossible, the sequence of stages by which the theatre took shape can be given tentatively in outline. The following account owes much to Fiechter, though modified considerably in the light of Pickard-Cambridge's more cautious conclusions ; one may say of it what Socrates in the *Phaedo* (114 D) says of his account of the soul's fate after death — no sensible person would insist that the facts are precisely so, but one may confidently assert that they are something after this fashion.[20]

In the sixth century there was an orchestra laid out on a terrace supported by a curved retaining wall, just above the old temple of Dionysus Eleuthereus at the south-eastern foot of the Acropolis. There may have been wooden seating on the slope, and perhaps a hut for the performers somewhere, but there was no place for a substantial skene. (The small theatre of the Attic deme Thoricus helps us to imagine what such a primitive arrangement was like ; the auditorium at Thoricus was irregular in outline and not curved into a semicircle but flattish, curving round at the ends. The orchestral area is not circular. There was no skene and no place for one, but on one side stood a small temple, and on the other a small building which may have been a *skenotheke* or store-room.[21])

Perhaps from the beginning a plain and simple background for the performances was sometimes used. As the fifth century advanced and Aeschylus produced his masterpieces and Sophocles his earliest plays, the pro-

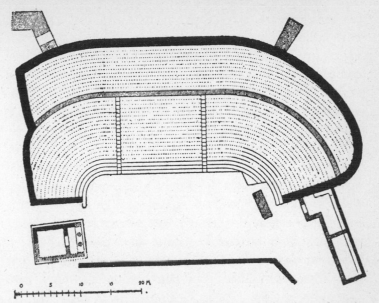

FIG. 44.   Theatre of Thoricus (Dörpfeld, *Das griechische Theater*, fig. 43)

ductions demanded a more imposing background, representing such buildings as a palace or a temple.   This was
provided by a skene presumably made of wood and
canvas ;   its arrangement could no doubt be varied a
good deal, in accordance with the requirements of particular plays ;   but since, when a stone skene came to be
built, the form with projecting wings or paraskenia was
chosen, it is reasonable to assume that this form had
already proved itself most serviceable and become normal.
After the middle of the fifth century, in the time of the
ascendancy of Pericles, there were further developments ;
the skene became more elaborate ;   in consequence the
orchestra had to be pushed a little further northward,
and in the process the auditorium must have been given
a steeper slope.   Possibly the provision of stone seating

for the audience was begun at this time. A stoa was built facing south over the shrine of Dionysus ; [22] this stoa formed a backing to the skene, which probably still consisted of wooden ' sets ', though Fiechter assigns the earliest stone skene to the Periclean reconstruction. The evidence — especially that of the plays themselves — is against a raised stage.[23]

In spite of the obscurity in which the fifth-century theatre is wrapped — perhaps to some extent because of it — one can at least be fairly sure that architectural maturity had not yet been attained. This was left for the fourth century, when the stone seating of the auditorium was completed and a stone skene erected, if indeed it had not been built in the latter part of the fifth century. The stone skene had projecting wings at either end, probably columnar, but its façade and its interior arrangement are quite uncertain. The fourth-century reconstruction is associated with the name of the statesman Lycurgus, about 330 B.C., but he may have done no more than finish the job. The orchestra was once again moved a little further north, and provided with the existing deep water-channel, which improved the drainage of the theatre and separated the orchestra more definitely from the auditorium. The theatre would now seat about 17,000. A raised stage is still improbable ; even a wooden structure cannot be proved to have existed.

It will be clear that the Athenian theatre grew piecemeal ; and not unnaturally it did not attain complete symmetry and regularity. From the fourth century onwards new theatres sprang up in large numbers, built as architectural units to a single main design ; to these the Athenian theatre stands in somewhat the same relation

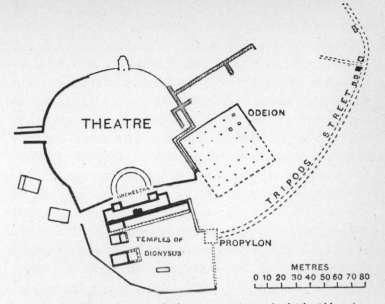

FIG. 45. Athens, theatre and adjacent monuments (Judeich, Abb. 39)

The small monuments along 'Tripods Street' were set up to celebrate victories in dramatic contests, and so were the two small buildings west of the theatre (left). The recess at the back of the auditorium is a small cave-sanctuary in the Acropolis rock, in front of which one Thrasyllus erected yet another 'choregic' monument in 319 B.C., in the form of a Doric porch.

as the city of Athens to Hippodamian cities. The irregular and broken outline of the auditorium is partly due to adjoining shrines and buildings, especially the Odeum of Pericles (built about 440 B.C.), a square columnar hall which itself served as a smaller covered theatre for musical contests and other purposes. The Dionysus theatre was also curiously linked with the surrounding parts of the city, and was less a self-contained unit than most theatres. It remained clearly a part, though a dominant part, of the shrine of Dionysus. The upper range of the auditorium extended across a public path which served in this section as the upper diazoma (the early auditorium was no doubt entirely below this level) ; and a 'street called Tripods' (Pausanias i. 20. 1), on which stood monuments of victories in the dramatic contests, led up to the theatre from the east after rounding the eastern end of the Acropolis.

By way of contrast with Athens, the theatre in the sanctuary of Asclepius at Epidaurus, the finest and best preserved in Greece, was planned by a single architect, the younger Polycleitus, in the fourth century. It illustrates perfectly the principles of design outlined above. The auditorium has the added refinement, both practical and aesthetic, that the upper range is pitched rather steeper. To Polycleitus' building belong the auditorium, the main body of the skene, and the elegant doorways across the parodoi. The *proskenion* is more problematical. It was a stone colonnade supporting a wooden platform level with the floor of the upper storey of the skene. It was probably a Hellenistic innovation ; though Bulle thinks that the ramps leading up to it on either side belonged to the original building and indicate a high wooden stage already in the fourth century.

In the Hellenistic age the stage-building attained its full architectural development, in several forms. The proskenion, introduced in the third century, became a regular feature.[24] Its height varied between 8 and 13 ft. It consisted either of pillars with engaged columns in front or of full columns, and panels were fitted in the intercolumnations. Proskenia were added to old theatres, the *paraskenia* losing prominence in the process. At Athens shallower colonnaded paraskenia were built, and a proskenion placed between them, in the second century

B.C. (according to Fiechter; this arrangement is dated by others later than the sack of Athens by Sulla in 86 B.C.). The proskenion was now normal in new theatres, which did not usually have paraskenia. Whether the proskenion was used regularly as a high stage right from the beginning, or only came to be so used in the second century, can probably never be finally decided; the experts still differ, though most favour the first alternative. Few believe with Dörpfeld that it remained a mere decorative background to the end. The use of a high stage is to be associated with the decline of the old chorus and the requirements of the Attic New Comedy of the late fourth and third centuries. From the beginning the form of the theatre was determined by the growing and changing needs of drama; but at many points it is only likely that there was a considerable and varying interval, due to religious conservatism and the expense of extensive rebuilding, before the needs were met and the change made. At Athens especially tradition was strong. Even after a high stage had become normal the orchestra was still used for certain types of performance.

Access to the proskenion platform was provided by a door or doors in the skene wall behind, and also, in a few theatres, by ramps at the sides, or, where the platform made a return round the ends of the skene, by stairs from the back. In the skene wall behind the platform the tendency was to introduce more and bigger openings, till in some cases the wall became little more than a series of pillars; these openings too could be filled with panels as the performances required.

As in the case of several other architectural types, in

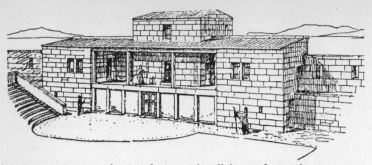

FIG. 46. New Pleuron, theatre and wall (E. Fiechter, *Theater von Neupleuron*, Pl. 8). (See VI, n. 16)

following out the development of the Greek theatre one is inevitably led into Hellenistic times before the tale can be considered complete. But beyond that there is no occasion to go. The Roman type of theatre, though it obviously owes a great deal to the Greek, is not merely a further stage on the same road. There is a definite break between the two. The Roman type involves different principles which may owe something to native Italian tradition. There is a stronger emphasis on stage and stage-building, which unites more closely with the auditorium, and the orchestra has little importance. In the Greek theatre the tradition of the simple archaic dancing-place was never wholly obliterated. The theatron and the skene stood on either side of the orchestra, focused upon it ; the three elements were brought into harmony, without attaining final unity.

VII

GREEK HOUSES [1]

THE Greek house is a fascinating but tantalizing subject. We would naturally like to form a clear picture of the setting in which the Greek spent his private life, but though here and there we get unobstructed and illuminating glimpses it would still be an understatement to say that there are large gaps in our knowledge. However, the evidence is now far greater and more reliable than when it was mainly drawn from somewhat obscure or even misleading accounts and references in ancient literature, especially since Olynthus has provided a good solid body of archaeological evidence for the late fifth and fourth centuries, to add to the later, mainly Hellenistic material. Several well developed house-types have emerged, bearing an interesting relation to one another ; but the possibility of a complete and systematic account of the Greek house is still remote ; it is impossible, for instance, to define which, if any, is the basic type and which are local variations. However, some features belong to all in common ; and in any case the unsolved problems do not vitally affect the question of the place of domestic architecture in the structure of the city.

Classical Greek houses were mostly unpretentious, at least from the outside ; they were hardly expected to make much contribution to the architectural beauty of the city ; and the layout of residential quarters was hardly ambitious. In the Minoan and Mycenean age the rulers' dwellings had been the highest achievements of architecture, containing within themselves all its most remarkable and characteristic elements. In the Hellenic city the functions of these great houses or palaces were distributed and diffused among a number of political and religious buildings, and house architecture was almost stripped of its monumental character ; even the prytaneion, in some ways the direct successor of the king's house, was usually quite simple. One may draw a contrast with domestic architecture in later ages too. The design of individual houses, and still more of groups of houses, streets and terraces, has sometimes been on the plane of the finest contemporary work. The Greeks of the fifth century put their best, architecturally, into temples and public buildings, and were content with modest private dwellings. Already in the fourth century the *laudatores temporis acti* were beginning to complain of a reversal of all this, probably without very good reason as yet. Even the best Hellenistic houses were elegant rather than magnificent, and for really elaborate and sumptuous establishments we have to wait till Roman times.

The modern planner pays particular attention to the residential parts of a town and makes it one of his principal aims to see that they are pleasant, healthy and convenient places to live in. In the scheme of the Greek city the houses were subordinate. The agora, the shrines, the theatre, gymnasia and so forth occupied sites determined by traditional sanctity or convenience. The houses filled in the rest. There was little possibility of a spacious layout or a generous allocation of ground.

The ordinary Greek urban house had little room for a domestic garden or for anything like the Italian garden-peristyle. The courtyard usually occupied only a small proportion of the area. Any tendency which there might have been towards a lavish use of space was ruled out by the need for compactness for purposes of defence. Narrow streets and houses huddled together, with sanitation rudimentary or non-existent, must have produced in large parts of most Greek cities conditions intolerable by modern standards ; and Athens seems to have been among the worst. The contrast between simple or even squalid domestic quarters and splendid public monuments is characteristic of classical Greece, where domestic affairs counted for less than political, social and religious life. But the divergence must not be exaggerated ; a typical house of the new quarter at Olynthus — or, one imagines, of a moderately well-to-do Athenian, not to speak of a Callias — was well designed and commodious *within itself*.[2] Given a good deal more breathing-space and equipped with good plumbing and the other ' magnificent alleviations of human destiny ' which have now become indispensable, such houses would not offend the best modern taste.

Even Olynthus does not quite give us the evidence we should most like to have, of a residential district in Athens or one of the other ancient cities of Greece in its best days. The Olynthian house-type may have been widespread in Greece, but the uniform rectangular blocks and parallel streets belong to a new era. However, the difference between old and new was perhaps not so very great, and the regularly planned cities, in which extensive residential areas, as opposed to isolated houses or small groups, have been fully investigated, can help the imagination a good deal in trying to picture the other kind, because in the layout of house-blocks as in other respects Hippodamian methods did not mean the introduction of entirely new elements, but rather a straightening out of the old. The streets being irregular in old towns, the house-blocks would not be uniform in size or shape ; but there would be the same compactness, which, combined with irregularity, would produce an effect of huddling ; and the same simplicity in external treatment and absence of calculated architectural effects in streets and groups of houses.[3] That a considerable number of houses might be united in a compact block is shown by such passages as Thucydides ii. 3, where the Plataeans use the method known now as 'mouse-holing' to avoid exposing themselves in the streets. Houses might also stand cheek by jowl with shrines (as in the archaic example from Aegina given below) or public buildings, or encroach on the agora occasionally (Timotheus' house at Peiraeus, Cleon's at Sicyon, the oligarchs' at Corcyra).[4] We can well believe that in unplanned towns the various ingredients, residential, political, religious, were more thoroughly mixed up. But to remind us again that the distinction is not so great, it may be noted that the Peiraeus example just given is from a Hippodamian town, and at Priene the 'Sacred House', where an unidentified cult was carried on, formed part of an ordinary house-block.

In Hippodamian towns the method of dealing with houses was simple and obvious. All the rectangular blocks not occupied by shrines or public buildings were available for houses, and each was divided up into a number of rectangular sites, usually but not always uniform in size. At Priene there is a good deal of variety in the way the blocks are divided. It is notable that there is no standardization of inner plan ; in fact, even on sites where streets and blocks are most rigidly laid out, within the limits set by the local type there is real individuality in the houses, and endless variety in the details of interior arrangement. There is a wide variation also between sites in the number of houses per block and their arrangement within the block, and in the size and proportions of the blocks.[5]

The evidence on many sites is very faulty and obscure. However, it appears that rectangles of very varied proportions were used, but never a perfect square. There were no hard and fast rules ; local convenience prevailed, if the choice was not purely arbitrary. Simple proportions and round figures were usual. The blocks at Priene measured 47·20 by 35·40 m. (160 by 120 ft. ; a proportion of 4 to 3). At Miletus the blocks are almost as large (51·60 by 29·50 m. ; 175 by 100 ft., *i.e.* 7 by 4), though this basic unit is sometimes cut into two parts, not always equal, by a cross-street.[6] At Olynthus a more elongated form is found — 300 by 120 ft. (5 by 2) — and a very narrow alley, probably intended mainly for drainage, divides the houses into two sets of five. Ten houses per block is an unusually large number ; Priene's four, and the proportions found at Priene, may perhaps be taken as more normal. A large house might occupy a whole block ; and occasionally two adjoining houses might be converted into one. Even as far as our very limited evidence goes, it is clear that there was endless local variety, and no general principles can be defined.

A brief account of the form of the Greek house will help to explain why it could make little positive contribution to the city's architectural scheme. At all times there must have been many houses consisting of very few rooms, perhaps one or two, without any distinctive plan or any architectural adornment. Houses of more ambitious form were always built round a small courtyard and looked inwards towards this rather than outwards towards the streets and their neighbours. Each was self-contained and turned in on itself. The entrance was inconspicuous and the windows usually placed high. Most of the rooms opened on to the courtyard. In certain types there was one dominant room which gave the impression of being the nucleus of the whole, and the other rooms and the courtyard itself appeared as appendages. In other types this emphasis was absent. The courtyard might have colonnades on one or several sides, or even be a complete and uniform peristyle (this last type, though hardly the normal classical form, was not purely Hellenistic). In any case, such architectural interest as the house offered was mainly concentrated in the interior. The exterior was plain and a street of such houses was unimpressive in its general effect, and aesthetically at least, little could be gained by giving it greater width.

The history of house architecture in Greece goes back to the earliest times of which we know. There are some elements which provide a tenuous but unbroken thread over a very long period. In particular, the so-called *megaron* persists and recurs. Perhaps it would be as well to define and explain this term at the outset, since we shall have to use it repeatedly. In classical literature it has several more or less related meanings ; in modern works on architecture it has come to be used for a particular type of building. This was essentially an oblong room or hall, deeper than it was wide, with an entrance on one of the short sides, usually through a porch formed by continuations of the walls of the long sides ; there might be an anteroom, or both porch and anteroom, and also a small back room. The rear end of the building might be apsidal or hairpin-shaped, though usually it was rectangular. There was sometimes a central hearth, and interior supports arranged in various ways, though normally with a longitudinal emphasis.[7] The megaron was essentially a northern form, suited to a comparatively cold and damp climate ; in architecture, as in other things, north met south and east in Greece.

Perhaps one should not say that there was a continuous development in house architecture in Greece but rather that history repeated itself several times. In the earliest prehistoric phases curvilinear and rectilinear forms existed side by side. It is impossible to show that the former are definitely more primitive, and unsafe to trace the evolution of the rectangular house from the circular hut by way of elliptical and apsidal forms. Curvilinear forms recur at later phases too ; they revive when civilization is at its ebb between the tides of Mycenean and Hellenic culture, but in classical Greek house-architecture they have been pretty well eliminated.

In Minoan and Mycenean times domestic architecture reached a very high degree. The great palaces are essentially highly elaborate forms of contemporary house-types. The difference between the Minoan palace, with its vast conglomeration of miscellaneous rooms around a large main court, and the Mycenean palace of the mainland, in which the great megaron dominates the courtyard, foreshadows the difference which we shall observe between two later Hellenic-Hellenistic types. In addition to the palaces, Minoan house architecture on a more modest scale was highly developed. But in this, as in other departments, it is impossible to determine to what extent the traditions of the land and the actual survival of remains influenced the rebirth of architecture in its Hellenic forms in the early centuries of the first millennium. At Thermon (see p. 106) it is claimed, and it is just possible, that the series of *megara* followed by temples forms an unbroken chain.

It would be very difficult and probably not very helpful to go to Homer for evidence of the Greek house. The picture he gives of the house or palace is ambiguous and open to various interpretations in many details and in general form — through no fault of the poet, of course — and it is impossible to say for what period he affords evidence. The Homeric royal house in the main seems to resemble the Mycenean ; it has a court-yard entered by a gateway, with colonnades on certain sides (there is no reason to assume a complete peristyle) ; a great hall and minor rooms opening on to the court, and subsidiary structures (hardly a duplicate court) at the back. To what extent royal residences of Mycenean or sub-Mycenean type were surviving or being built or rebuilt in the early centuries of the first millennium one cannot say. Homer at least shows that knowledge of the type, or something like it, persisted. The remains, or their absence, suggest that architecture went back to modest beginnings again.

The rectangular megaron probably survived — it is found again in some of the early archaic house-models described below — but elliptical and apsidal forms were also employed again. A curious example is an elliptical house of whose walls sections have been found in what was later the agora at Athens, at the south end ; [8] it measured about 11 m. by 5 m. ; its interior arrangement is uncertain, but there was probably a hearth near the middle. The house is assumed to have had a thatched roof, crowning a wall built of unbaked brick on a lower part of small stones.

In the period of ' geometric ' art (ninth and eighth centuries), to which this house belongs, when Hellenic architecture was beginning to emerge, house and temple are hardly to be distinguished. The temple was the dwelling of a god, and in form would be like a simple house, or the main part of a house. It has been plausibly conjectured that the building called ' Megaron B ' at Thermon, which also belongs to the geometric period, began as a house and ended as a temple. In quite early archaic times (seventh century) house and temple parted company, the latter to develop on monumental lines. The small models of buildings, of which we have an interesting series belonging to the eighth century or thereabouts, have sometimes been called temples, but some are more probably houses — the form of the roof seems to indicate that it contained a sort of attic or upper storey. In the chief model from Perachora, near Corinth, the sides converge slightly towards the back, where they end in an apse. The side walls end at the front in *antae* ; in front of one of the latter stand two columns close together side by side ; and another pair can be presumed in front of the other *anta*, forming a prostyle porch. The roof, which can be restored with the help of fragments of other models, was steep and slightly curved, and the gable at the front was open. It is assumed that the roof in such a house would be of thatch, and this is borne out by the twist which runs along the crest. The models from the shrine of Hera, near Argos, were similar in general, but were rectangular, and had two single columns in place of the Perachora pairs. There seems to have been a flat ceiling, which might have served as a floor for an upper storey (this was probably the case in the Perachora examples too), and the front gable contains a large square opening. It will be observed that these ' houses ' are more or less megaron-like ; but a model from Samos is elliptical, with a door towards the end of one side. The models would be dedicated to the deity in whose shrines they were found. They give us a curiously vivid glimpse of the architecture of a period for which most of the evidence has been quite obliterated. But they hardly tell the whole tale. Presumably there were houses of more complicated plan ; or a court and minor rooms might be attached to a main structure of the kind shown in the models.

For the seventh and even the sixth century material is scantier than ever. There are slight remains of houses on a number of sites, but as a rule it is impossible to determine the plan, and at best there is little sign of the establishment of well-marked types. As an example may be mentioned a small group of sixth-century houses at Aegina, built over the remains of a prehistoric fortress palace. They stood close to the temple of Aphrodite; in fact they were built over later when the shrine was enlarged. They contained two or three rooms opening on to a small walled court.[9] One at least departed very markedly from strictly rectangular form. A narrow street divides the group. Thus we have here a curious fragment of an archaic town, with houses standing immediately by an important shrine.[10]

Until Olynthus was excavated evidence for the fifth and fourth centuries was not much more plentiful than for archaic times and consisted mainly of vague literary allusions. Imaginary plans of the typical Greek house used to be drawn, which were usually correct in grouping the rooms about a courtyard, but wrong in giving them symmetry about an axis ; this is a principle which was foreign to the classical Greek house, as far as we can tell, and more characteristic of the Italian, as seen at Pompeii. This perfect symmetry was emphasized in some reconstructions by duplicating the courtyard, with peristyle, surrounding rooms and all ; the assumption was that the one court was the men's quarters, the other the women's. But such reconstructions were based on doubtful interpretations of the literary evidence, particularly on Vitruvius,[11] whose descriptions of Greek building-types have often been the reverse of helpful if taken to apply to times much earlier than his own. The ' Greek house ' which he describes is one of extreme luxury, rare in Greece in the fifth and fourth centuries, and indeed at any time. The monuments show that the reconstructions with duplicate courts are not only false but contrary to the whole spirit of the true Greek house. We shall come across one or two specimens with two courts, but they are not symmetrical and perfectly balanced. And Greek houses certainly contained something which was called the *gynaikonitis*,[12] or women's quarters, but it was probably not of such extent or form as to have a radical effect on the whole design of the house.

We can well believe that most houses in the fifth century were simple in plan and inexpensive in equipment. There must have been many small nondescript houses at Athens. Most of the slight and scattered remains of the period are of this kind. But Demosthenes (iii. 25) is presumably exercising some rhetorical licence when he says that the houses of the leading citizens were in no way distinguishable from the rest. We read of houses being sold for high prices. We are told of comparatively luxurious country houses in Attica. The well-known scene of the opening of Plato's *Protagoras* gives a vivid if vague impression of the house of one of the wealthiest Athenians, Callias. Socrates and his friend first stand talking in a porch outside the door. When finally admitted they find themselves in a court-yard with at least two colonnades ; probably there would be an altar in the courtyard, as in Polemarchus' house (*Republic* 328) ; rooms opened on to the court ; one was a bedroom — Prodicus was still in bed — but it had only been pressed into service because Callias had so many guests, and was normally a store-room ; the ordinary bedrooms would, perhaps, be upstairs. These are illuminating touches but they leave us in the dark about the extent of the house and the principles of its plan. A remarkable specimen of a fairly large and elaborate fifth-century house is known at Dystus in Euboea. It is rectangular, with some irregularities, and has two courts, the outer entered by a long passage with two doors, running along the side of the house. The house was two-storeyed and contained a number of rooms arranged on no clear principle. The courtyards had no colonnades, though one large room opened on to the inner court through a row of three pillars. This house was also superior to most in that it was built mainly of stone. Unburnt brick on a low stone socle may be taken to be the usual technique at this time.

At Olynthus we are at last on firm ground. Not only does the site provide a mass of archaeological material but it also reveals a distinctive and apparently well-established house-type. The plan must have been the product of some sort of evolution, but where and when this took place, and over what areas the Olynthian type was prevalent, it is impossible to say. The houses with which we are chiefly concerned were built on the north hill of Olynthus. The south hill was occupied by the older part of the town, and on it have been found remains of small houses of poorer class, irregularly built. There are also one or two superior houses at Olynthus, of a type similar to the main body on the north hill but more elaborate, standing somewhat aloof. There was apparently some residential segregation of classes at Olynthus. Whether this was at all general is doubtful. On the whole it is not likely that in the old cities there were definitely poorer- and richer-class districts ; probably in this as in other respects, the elements were fairly well mixed. And in new Hippodamian towns the method of planning did not make for a strong differentiation of districts ; in a city like Priene there is a certain uniformity about the whole. It is not to be imagined that in any Greek city there would be the complete difference in atmosphere which there is in a modern city between the well-to-do suburbs and poor quarters huddled together in the centre ; this difference is largely the result of the ability of the modern town to spread itself indefinitely.

The development of the north hill at Olynthus did not begin before the middle of the fifth century, perhaps not till 432 B.C.. The houses were built between that date and 348, when Olynthus was destroyed by Philip of Macedon ; it is seldom possible to date individual houses more precisely within the period ; we may take them as representative of the late fifth and early fourth century. The quarter was laid out on strictly rectangular lines ; the arrangement of the houses in blocks of ten has already been mentioned (p. 179 ; see fig. 5). The houses are roughly square and were divided into approximately equal north and south parts. The northern part consisted of a long narrow room, the so-called *pastas*,[13] extending across the whole or nearly the whole of the house ((*f*) in fig. 47), with a series of other rooms opening on to it from the north. In the middle of the south side was a small court, usually cobbled and sometimes containing a cistern and an altar (of Zeus, God of the Courtyard). The court might have colonnades on other sides besides the pastas, and several had a small peristyle complete. There was seldom much more than a mere wall on the south side of the court. The pastas opened on to the court through a row of three or four pillars. The house thus faced mainly south, in accordance with the wise recommendation of ancient writers,[14] turning its back on the north wind and catching the winter sun. This was so even in the houses on the north side of the

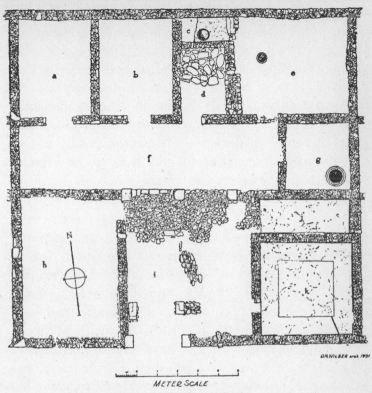

FIG. 47. House at Olynthus (*Olynthus*, viii, Pl. 100)

block. The entrance was contrived in a great variety of ways; usually there was only one, but some houses had two; the door was sometimes flush with the outer wall, sometimes in a recess (*prothyron*). The houses contained no dominant room, as at Priene, which could be said to form a nucleus; as the excavators say, 'The underlying principle is one of growth by division rather than by accretion'. The most distinctive feature is the pastas, after which the Olynthian house-type has been named. Other rooms on the ground floor numbered usually about five to seven ; but the house of Zoilus in the same area contrives to include a total of seventeen. Often the rooms are impossible to identify ; the main dining- and enter-taining-room (andron) (k) was distinguished by a low raised platform round the walls on which couches would rest, more elaborate wall decoration,[15] and a cemented or occasionally a pebble-mosaic floor — most rooms had floors of hard-packed earth. The andron usually had an ante-room so arranged as to give it a certain privacy, and the two may have constituted the andronitis or men's quarters. There was apparently no elaborate provision for separate women's quarters in the Olynthian houses. Many of the houses contained a closely connected group of three rooms, one large and two small ; the large room (e) was a living- and work-room, the centre of the ordinary workaday life of the house ; sometimes it had a fixed hearth in the middle, constructed of stone slabs, though movable braziers were also used. A small bathroom frequently opened off it (c). The third room (d) is more problematical. It was first identified by the excavators as a flue for the living-room, but further examination has shown that it was something more, a small kitchen, in fact, though it may have been continued upwards as a flue. Store-rooms and work-rooms are identified in some cases by their contents. The houses were too small to need a porter's lodge as did the house of Callias and some Delian houses. Some had a narrow paved room which may have been a stable. Bedrooms were presumably on the upper floor, the existence of which, in some houses at least, is proved by traces of stairs leading up from the courtyard, usually to the northern part of the house.[16] The houses were built of unbaked brick, which may have had a protective coating, on a foundation of rubble, with considerable use of wood, of course — the pillars were mostly wooden — and terra-cotta tiles for the sloping roofs. For water supply, apart from occasional cisterns, the inhabitants must have depended on the city fountains. There were no effective sanitary arrangements.

A remarkable feature of these houses is their variety. There was a standard size and shape at Olynthus, but internal arrangement differed widely. No two houses were the same, even though they conformed strictly to the plan and were built in closely knit units of five (*i.e.* half-blocks). The court, though essential, was sometimes reduced to diminutive proportions. The characteristic pastas was often broken up and obscured, and occasionally even omitted ; once at least one pastas was carried right across two houses, which clearly belonged to one family. Several normal square house-units were divided into two dwellings or several sets of rooms. Often there were shops opening on the street — usually one of the main north-south avenues — and not communicating with the house behind. All this variety shows how the Greek citizen, while fitting into his place as a member of the polis, could assert a lively individuality.

Thus at Olynthus we have a large group of well-planned houses, designed for families of moderate means and a taste for comfort without extravagance. One would like to feel that they fairly represent the fifth- and fourth-century Greek house, and since they have as strong a claim as any to do so, I have described them in some detail ; but one cannot be sure. This pastas type is clearly well established, since it is employed in such a regular and well-developed form and on such a scale. There are several other sporadic examples of the pastas-house, mainly later than Olynthus, and some of the larger Hellenistic houses of Delos combine pastas with peristyle. How far the influence of various types extended in space and time is impossible to say. The excavators of Olynthus tentatively suggest that a form which was prevalent at Olynthus and found at Delos is not likely to have been unknown at Athens ; and that of the two the Priene type is more likely to have been local and limited in range.

A small group of interesting fourth-century houses has been examined at Colophon in Ionia.[17] They were irregular and each was arranged loosely round an inner yard containing a well and an altar. The chief part of the house, consisting of a main room and porch, as at Priene, and subordinate rooms opening off them, was on the north. Somewhat detached from this block was an important and well-decorated room which was probably the andron or men's entertaining room ; above it was a second storey which may have been the gynaikonitis, forming a *pyrgos* or tower. Store-rooms, stables and so forth occupied the rest of the sides of the court. The whole was loosely compacted as compared with the houses of Olynthus and Priene, as if it had not yet firmly coalesced into a single unit.

Priene provides a large body of evidence for another Greek house-type, though again it is impossible to define precisely the part this played in the history of domestic architecture. The houses of Priene are themselves mainly Hellenistic. Their most striking feature is the reappearance of a megaron-like arrangement as the basis of the plan. The main room of the house, which is usually on the north side facing south, is of megaron form, with usually a columnar porch in front (the *pro-*

stas, after which the type has been called to distinguish it from the pastas variety). The courtyard seems to be a forecourt to this main structure and the subordinate rooms opening on several or all sides of the court appear as accretions. This emphasis on one element and sub-ordination of the rest give the best Priene houses a more monumental character than the Olynthian, as does also the increased use of stone — Hellenistic houses in general show improved technique. Traces of stairs show that there were second storeys, though one cannot say whether this was so in all houses or in all parts of a particular house. Complete peristyle courts were not introduced at Priene until a late phase ; the house num-bered 33, for instance, was re-designed with a peristyle, of the kind called Rhodian by ancient architects, with the north colonnade higher than the rest (it is found at Delos too) ; house 33 also joined up with its neigh-bour and acquired a second court. Most of the houses had an entrance porch set back from the street. As at Olynthus, within the general type there is a great deal of variety in the number and arrangement of rooms. One or two houses have two megaron-like rooms side by side, perhaps one for men and one for women.

In these houses the megaron form, after maintaining what was probably a precarious existence for some cen-turies, emerges strongly again. There is no reason to believe that the megaron had played a dominant part in Greek house architecture right through. It had had a long and notable history and had perpetuated one variety of itself in the temple ; in the house it was not an essential element, but perhaps rather a survival. Olynthus and Delos, as compared with Priene, lose nothing for practical purposes by dispensing with it.

There is no need to describe in detail the well-known Hellenistic houses of Delos. It will be sufficient to indicate briefly the type which is most characteristic of Delos and to emphasize several points which are significant for the planning of a residential quarter. In spite of its typically Hellenistic elements, Delos may help us in some ways towards a clearer picture of the residential streets of a Hellenic city. In the first place, houses of very varied size and elaboration are found huddled together in the same quarter, sometimes even in the same block. The better houses had a considerable number of rooms, some of them spacious and richly adorned, built round an elegant peristyle court. This type naturally has received most attention and is apt to be thought of as most distinctively Delian. But there were many poorer, simpler houses. The site on which most of the houses were built is irregular, sloping and rocky ; and the narrow streets are very irregular, though Priene shows that such conditions did not necessarily prevent the uncompromising application of Hippodamian planning. Blocks and individual houses were extremely varied in shape ; this meant that many rooms were of strange and awkward design ; but there was a tendency to smooth out the irregularities in the inner part of the house. Even so, in some cases the walls of the court were still not quite rectangular, and regularity was only attained in the columns of the peristyle. A peristyle is not invariably found even in the larger Delian houses, but it occurs even in the third century, to which the earliest Delian houses of this group belong. In some cases it was not an original feature of the court but a later insertion. The court was usually on the south side, so that once again the houses mainly turn south-wards. There is usually only one entrance, into the courtyard through a narrow passage or vestibule ; but a few houses have two. The rooms are seldom placed on more than three sides of the court. Often there is one large richly decorated room which is clearly the main room of the house; it is not of the megaron type as at Priene, but broad and comparatively shallow ; sometimes it has small inner rooms opening off it at the back. In general, the houses are more closely related to those of Olynthus than of Priene ; in a house like the ' Maison de la Colline ', which is nearly square and unusually regular, and in which extensions of the north colonnade of the house form a room like the Olynthian pastas stretching right across the house, the resemblance is very marked. There is more evidence at Delos than elsewhere for the upper storey, which was often very ornate. Occasionally there was an exterior stairway to the upper floor, which may then be assumed to have formed a separate ' flat '.[18] In the ' theatre street ' and elsewhere there were rooms which opened on the street and had no communication with the houses into which they were built ; these were shops.

The houses of Delos were mostly inhabited by more or less prosperous merchants at a time when Delos was a great commercial centre. Lining the quays there were buildings of similar plan, with rooms around a columned court, which are assumed to have been ware-houses. The basic Greek house-type could very easily be adapted to various purposes and serve as inn, fac-tory or school. Delos provides a curious bit of further

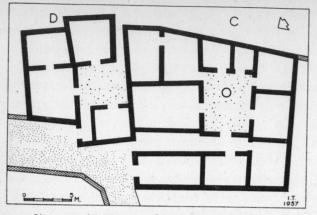

FIG. 48. Fifth century houses west of Areopagus, Athens (Travlos, fig. 34)
see p. 228

evidence. Inscriptions mention farm-buildings, giving lists of their constituent elements ; [19] there are various rooms, and stalls for cattle, apparently grouped round a courtyard, since the 'door to the courtyard' is repeatedly mentioned. A house could also contain workshops and factories. Remains of simple houses have been found on the west side of the agora at Athens in which potters and bronze workers carried on their trade. Lysias, who had an arms factory, gives a glimpse of a bigger establishment ; he describes how, when the representatives of the Thirty came to his house, some arrested him as he was entertaining guests, while others seized the slaves in the workshop (xii. 8).

It would be unsafe to make any further generalizations than we have already made about the form of the Greek house. The evidence still clearly consists of nothing more than scraps ; and Olynthus shows that the material from a single new site may make it necessary to revise theories and preconceived ideas. One can only repeat that the Greek house, when it attained any distinctive plan at all, was built round an interior court ; it looked in on this and it turned mainly south-wards. Endless variations on this scheme were possible. The arrangement of rooms was generally informal and free from strict symmetry.

Prostas, simple pastas, and pastas with peristyle have been taken to be distinguishing marks of different types, but the distinction between them is not really funda-mental, as it is between all these types and the kind of house in which we in north-west Europe now live. The origin and interrelation of the known varieties of Greek house are difficult and, I think, not very profitable sub-jects for our present purposes. It has been maintained that the megaron with forecourt, that is the Priene variety, is the original type, and that foreign influences, Egyptian and oriental, tend to oust the megaron and put in its place the peristyle house. But it cannot be shown that the megaron ever had to be ousted, or that it ever dominated Greek house-architecture. In any case its abandonment was a natural step ; a megaron was not indispensable to a classical Greek house. Nor need one doubt that all the types we know grew on Greek soil through native inven-tion without foreign importations. Take the peristyle in particular, which is said to be foreign to Greece ; [20] it is allowed that the true Greek house might have several separate colonnades on different sides of the court ; it was not beyond the inventiveness of Greek architects to see that these might be made into a complete and regular square ; and rectangular planning, as we have seen in the case of the agora, tended to foster the combination of stoas into rectangular schemes.

VIII

FOUNTAIN BUILDINGS [1]

FOUNTAIN-HOUSES, which were both public monuments and necessities of domestic life, deserve a place in any account of the Greek city's architectural scheme. If I conclude with a brief appendix on them, it is not merely because I am committed to working through Pausanias' list (p. xix). They were of vital importance and received special care. Ancient writers frequently include them among the interesting features and adornments of a city. Pausanias, besides adding them to his list of essential elements, shows a marked interest in fountains, their architectural form and the quantity and quality of their water. Secondly, they illustrate particularly well the severe restraint of Greek architecture, the way in which, in all their efforts to achieve beauty, the architects kept a firm hold on the practical and the functional. Fountains make a very natural appeal to the artistic imagination ; and in other ages artists have often let their fancies run riot in designing architecture and sculpture for them. With the Greeks it was quite the contrary. Apart from artistic principles, water supply was a serious, often desperately serious, matter, increasingly so as cities outgrew their original supplies. Efficient governments gave much thought to it ; there were special magistrates, of high standing, appointed to take care of the fountains.

Greek towns were largely dependent on water available in the immediate neighbourhood, or indeed within the walls. There would be serious disadvantages in bringing copious supplies from more or less distant hills by aqueducts. This was not altogether due to deficiency of technique. Considerable aqueducts, constructed with great technical skill, *were* made before Hellenistic and Roman times ; not of course great monumental structures striding over the countryside on arches, but mainly underground conduits, concealed for safety, with strong carefully fitted terra-cotta pipes in rock-cut or masonry channels. The tunnel of Eupalinus at Samos, which Herodotus (iii. 60. 1) regarded with such wonder, was a great feat of engineering ; at Athens the tyrants built an aqueduct to supply the city, and Meton at the end of the fifth century built one to Peiraeus. At Olynthus a very fine specimen has been found, designed to bring water to a city fountain from hills several miles to the north, and showing a knowledge of engineering which few would have attributed to the Greeks before Hellenistic times. The expense involved was a hindrance to the construction of such large aqueducts, but most decisive was the political state of Greece ; such methods imply settled conditions over a wide area and are unreliable for a city which is frequently at war with its neighbours and from time to time closely besieged. The conditions established by the Roman Empire made possible the construction of many great aqueducts, and the use of the arch on a grand scale made their visible sections rank among the finest architectural achievements of antiquity. The architectural types associated with water-supply in pre-Roman Greece are much more modest but no less characteristic.

Greece is, in any case, poor in water, and when in

addition the circumstances were as described, extreme care was necessary to make the best of the water available on the site; numerous wells were sunk and cisterns cut in the rock to collect rain water. Wells and cisterns, in contrast to the public fountains, might belong to private houses. Their water would be of doubtful quality and purity. Springs and fountains were objects of public care and indeed veneration; very often they had religious and legendary associations, to which their names bear witness. They were the chief source of pure water; the users brought their pitchers and filled them from the spouts and basins. The supply was not normally conducted to individual houses; though conduits were used a good deal to bring the water from its source to convenient sites. At present I am not concerned with technical details of the provision and distribution of water, but rather with such parts of the system as contributed to the city's architecture, though it is difficult to draw the line clearly. In designing these, architects kept in mind certain practical aims — to catch and conserve the water, to make it easily accessible for public use, and to keep it cool and clean.

The existence of copious springs of wholesome water was an important factor in determining where villages and cities should grow. A citadel, too, if it was to be able to stand a long siege, needed a good spring; so we find the upper Peirene on the Acrocorinthus, and Klepsydra on the north-west slope of the Acropolis of Athens. The same factor counted for a good deal in deciding what sites within a city should be developed as agora, gymnasia and so forth. An important fountain is often found in close association with the agora. In the main Nature decided. The natural source, however, was sometimes some little distance from the artificial fountain. In fact the two occasionally had different names ; the fountain Arsinoe at Messene was fed from a spring called Klepsydra (Pausanias iv. 31. 6). Fountains occur in a great variety of places : in streets, in shrines and tucked away in odd corners — for instance, the Dipylon fountain at Athens was built into an angle of the great gate. The agora, as has been said, commonly has a fountain (or several); this fact inclines one to believe that Enneakrounos, *the* fountain of Athens (p. 57), was in or near the agora, not away to the south-east of the city, other arguments in this notorious problem of Athenian topography being evenly balanced. These agora fountains were not ornamental centre-pieces but located and designed for convenient use.

' A spring of bright water flows from beneath a cave, and round it poplars grow ', says Homer (*Odyssey* ix. 140), describing a fountain left presumably in its natural state. The simplest artificial treatment consisted of dressing the living rock. As in other classes of building, the Greeks let nature build for them, and simply modified her work and finished the job. The rock-face could be hewn to a smooth surface, and basins hollowed out from which the water could be drawn, and long deep cisterns, sometimes several lying parallel, driven back into the rock to act as reservoirs. This was the most appropriate scheme when the fountain-house was constructed against a rocky terrace or slope. When the water welled up in a hollow, steps might be cut down to a basin. Sometimes the spring was in a cave or grotto which could easily be adapted as a well-house. A num-

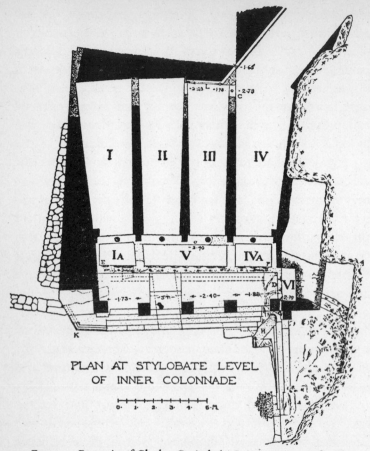

FIG. 49. Fountain of Glauke, Corinth (*A.J.A.*, 1910, p. 19, fig. 2)

ber of fountain-houses, including some important archaic examples, are mainly rock-hewn ; probably in their original form they had little if any added architectural ornament, though it is sometimes difficult to be sure because of later and more elaborate rebuildings. Glauke at Corinth is an excellent example of the rock-cut fountain-house ; probably Peirene (lower) too in its early form; later both acquired increasingly handsome columnar façades. On the other hand, another early fountainhouse, the one which the tyrant Theagenes (late seventh century) built at Megara and adorned with many columns (Pausanias i. 40. 1), though of similar general plan (*i.e.* with long parallel cisterns behind and narrow drawbasins in front), was constructed largely of masonry, and the roof of the cisterns was supported by columns.

Theagenes' building shows that even in early archaic times elaborate fountain-houses were made. The tyrants of the late seventh and sixth centuries were particularly fond of them. Peirene and Glauke [2] at Corinth are generally attributed to Periander ; and Thucydides tells (ii. 15) how the tyrants at Athens converted the spring Kallirrhoe into the fountain Enneakrounos. The change of name is significant ; ' Kallirrhoe ' (Fair-flowing) suits a source left in its natural state, and Thucydides says that the springs were originally visible ; ' Enneakrounos ' (Nine-spouted) speaks of a more artificial treatment.

The addition of a columnar porch was a natural and early development. It gave the city fountains dignity and conformity with other public buildings. The ' spring flowing from beneath a cave ', even if the rock was laboriously hewn and shaped, was out of place in more sophisticated surroundings. But the columnar porch was not a mere façade or veneer ; it served the useful purposes of protecting the water and keeping it pure, and giving shade and shelter to those who came to draw ; and it did not disguise the nature of the fountain. Very rarely, as in the Troilus pediment from the Acropolis (early sixth century),[3] was the fountain enclosed within four walls.

Vase-paintings often show fountain-houses, particularly in the sixth century, and indicate that a number of forms of varying complexity continued in existence side by side from early times. The painters have their own shorthand or impressionistic methods of representing things, and caution is needed in translating their pictures into three-dimensional architectural forms. But it is clear that the fountain-houses were mainly small columnar buildings, prostyle or *in antis* ; the water flowed from spouts in the back wall (*i.e.* the front wall of the basin or cistern if there is one), or sometimes in the side walls too ; sometimes the spout is high enough to provide a shower. Naturally the vase-painters insert spouts with water flowing from them, since this makes the nature of the scene clearer. In some real fountains the water was obtained by dipping pitchers over the parapet into the basin ; or both methods might be used. *Milet* (i. 5) gives a series of possible plans of which most

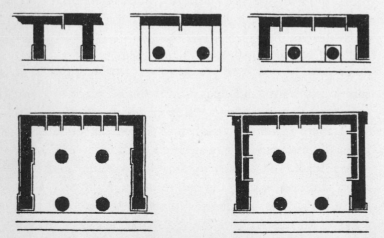

Fig. 50. Plans of typical fountain-houses (from *Milet*, i. 5)

are found in actual fountain-houses ; Miss Dunkley thinks that those schemes which have spouts pouring out on either side of a single wall did not exist in real fountains, but were invented by artists to make a symmetrically arranged scheme (she also believes that what appear to be solid pillars with spouts attached are in fact conventional representations of the outer wall of a cistern).

Architectural details are sketchy and obscure in the vase-paintings. The floor consists of one or several steps. The columns are generally very slender. This may be merely an artistic convention ; but perhaps this and other details indicate that wood was used in minor structures like these after stone had become normal in temples. Variations in the treatment of the entablature too may also indicate that the builders allowed themselves more freedom than was possible in major works of architecture, in which the conventions of the orders, once established, were more strictly preserved. Few of the fountain-houses on vases have pediments, but this may only mean that the artists usually stopped short here.

The rarer sunken-basin type of fountain received architectural embellishment too. Steps and parapets of masonry were built. An elaborate version is found in a fountain at Delos, probably called Minoe. Stone steps led down to a square basin. The whole was enclosed and covered by means of a colonnade in front and a wall round the back and the greater part of the sides. A single column in the middle on one of the steps provided central support for a roof which may have been pyramidal. The columns were perhaps originally wooden,

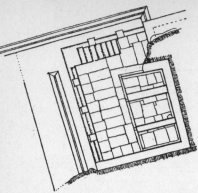
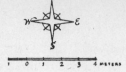

FIG. 51. Fountain Klepsydra, Athens (restored plan, after
A. W. Parsons in *Hesperia*, xii, p. 253, fig. 30)

later replaced by stone ; and the original date was probably the end of the fifth century.

The historic fountain of Klepsydra on the north-west
slope of the Acropolis at Athens has recently been carefully investigated. Welling up in a deep cleft, it was in
use from remote prehistoric times, but an artificial spring-
house was not constructed till the fifth century, soon after
the Persian Wars. A deep rectangular basin of well-
fitted masonry was inserted like a box into the cleft.
Steps at the north-west corner led down to a paved
platform which enclosed the basin on west and north ;
and users descended to this to lower their vessels over a
railing into the water. The native rock of the roof caved
in in the first century A.D., and some time later a well-
house with circular shaft was constructed on top of the
debris, completely obscuring the old fountain-house.
Strangely, it was not until this rebuilding, late in the
second century A.D., that Klepsydra was made directly
accessible from the top of the Acropolis and its use
secured to the garrison. Until then, the defenders had

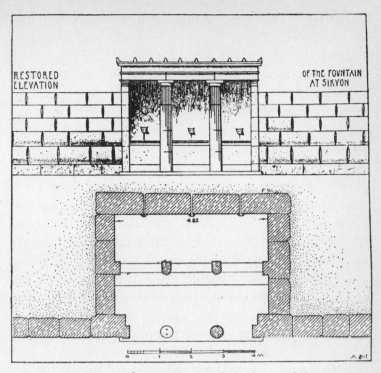

FIG. 52. Fountain-house at Sicyon, plan and restored elevation
(*A.J.A.*, 1934, Pl. XVI)

had to rely largely on cisterns, constructed in great
numbers at various dates.

It is impossible to classify Greek fountain-houses
precisely. They do not conform closely to types and
there are many peculiar specimens; but from the middle
of the fourth century a particular type established itself
as normal; in this there are oblong draw-basins with
a parapet in front and possibly cisterns extending behind.
Columns or piers are placed on the parapet wall, or built
into it, to support the roof, and there is a colonnade in

front too. The type continues into Hellenistic and Roman times. There is an excellent and well-preserved example at Ialysos in Rhodes, dated in the fourth century; and there are two simpler specimens, belonging to the end of the fourth century, in a gymnasium at Sicyon.

Greek fountains are almost devoid of fanciful ornament. Apart from the normal architectural forms, decoration is almost confined to the spouts. Often, of course, there would be statues near by, particularly of the appropriate deities, and as always these were meant to be seen in relation to their architectural setting. Spouts are placed in the front wall of the basins in convenient places for the users to fill their pitchers (sometimes there are raised steps on which these can be set), and in the back wall, leading from the cisterns and the source behind. By far the most common form of spout is the lion's head; in fact others may be regarded as mere exceptions. Some plain tubular spouts are found, and a few heads or foreparts of other animals, and there are one or two complete lions. But the lion's head, sometimes in bronze, more often in stone, was thought most appropriate; the spreading mane offered a broad base for firm attachment. In designing outlets for water the artist obviously has great scope for ingenuity; and in some ages full advantage has been taken of this. Now and then a touch of fancy was permitted in the Greek fountains; for instance, on a lion-head spout from Samos a humorous sculptor carved a small frog.

The surplus water from spouts and basins was sometimes collected again in a further open basin in front of the fountain before being finally allowed to flow away. Sometimes the overflow was conducted away in channels to some suitable place ; good spring water was too precious to be lightly wasted. Occasionally the stream served another fountain lower down.

The form of these Greek fountain-buildings — simple, dignified and restrained, based on the natural character of the spring and the convenience of its users — can be emphasized by contrast with the ornate and tasteless structures which were built in Greece in Roman imperial times. The Nymphaeum at Miletus is a good example. The essentials are still the same ; the water is brought to the site by an aqueduct ; there are cisterns behind and large open basins in front ; but all this is made the occasion for a lavish display of decorative architecture. An enormous columnar façade in three storeys encloses the main basin along the back and sides (the earlier Greek fountain-houses never have several storeys). The basin is not even covered and protected, but this is unimportant since it is merely part of the decorative scheme. In niches on the façade are innumerable figures of gods and nymphs and portraits of human beings. The elements of the Greek fountain are still there, but the spirit is sadly changed.

NOTES

INTRODUCTION

1. I have not said any more about the cemeteries below, and they deserve a little more notice. The finest of them contributed a good deal to the embellishment of the city's outer fringe ; but many others were simple plots of ground. A few very distinguished individuals, almost raised to semi-divine status along with legendary heroes and founders, were buried in the agora or elsewhere within the city. For good and contrasting examples of recently investigated cemeteries see : (1) G. Karo, *An Attic Cemetery* (Philadelphia, 1943) (Karo summarizes the results of investigations in the outer Kerameikos at Athens, outside the Dipylon, the main gate on the north-west ; this was the chief cemetery of Athens, and contained a fine series of sculptured monuments of the sixth to fourth centuries, some of which rank with the best art of their time) ; (2) *Olynthus*, vol. xi (this deals with the cemeteries of Olynthus, and incidentally with Greek cemeteries and burial in general ; the Olynthian cemeteries were more modest affairs and probably more typical of the ordinary Greek cemetery ; the simple graves were huddled together, with very few monuments ; in many the body was covered with several large tiles, and there is an appalling proportion of small children's graves, in which a large jar is generally used to contain the body. One handsome chamber-tomb, however, has been discovered at Olynthus, apart from the rest.)

I. GROWTH OF THE GREEK CITY

1. A. von Gerkan's *Griechische Städteanlagen* (Berlin and Leipzig, 1924) is still the main authority on the subject. Fabricius' article in Pauly-Wissowa, II. Reihe, Halbb. 6, cols. 1982 ff. (1929), supplements and summarizes, and has a good bibliography. F. Haverfield's *Ancient Town-Planning* still makes an interesting introduction, though it is out of date. F. Tritsch, 'Die Stadtbildungen des Altertums und die griechische Polis' (*Klio*, xxii, 1928, pp. 1-83), is important. There is a recent brief treatment of the subject, from an architect's point of view, by R. Martiensen in *South African Architectural Review*, Jan. 1941.

2. *Klio*, 1928, p. 76.

3. Von Gerkan, pp. 4-6.

    I. Gradual formation through naturally favourable conditions.

        (1) Towns developed from simple villages, without Mycenean forerunners (especially in the west of Greece proper, Epirus, Arcadia, Elis, Achaia).

(2) Towns which were a continuation of Mycenean settlements, the latter acting as 'crystallization-points'; these include many of the greatest cities of Greece, among them Athens.

II. Foundation through the arbitrary act of a founder or group of founders, to meet some special need.

(1) Capital chosen for a state formed by synoecism (political unification of several communities).

(a) Town already existing chosen, which would now develop rapidly; Athens, later Tegea and Elis.

(b) Younger form of synoecism, by which part of the population of the participating towns was brought together in a new city on new ground; Megalopolis, Rhodes.

(2) Colonization.

(a) Older colonies, begun in early wanderings of Greek peoples; Miletus, Ephesus.

(b) Later colonies; more deliberate and organized.

4. Aristophanes in the *Birds* makes Meton draw a plan for a real 'Place de l'Étoile' for Nephelococcygia, the city in the clouds; '. . . in the centre A market-place; and streets are leading to it Straight to the very centre; just as from A star, though circular, straight rays flash out In all directions' (1005-9, Rogers' translation). But there is nothing like this in the real planned towns we know. The scene is farcical. If the idea is to be taken seriously at all, it is the brain-wave of an amateur, suggested by the roughly radial form of old towns, not based on the methods of practising experts.

5. *Klio*, 1928, p. 64.

6. A. W. Gomme, *Population of Athens* (Blackwell, 1933); for other statistics see G. Glotz, *The Greek City* (1929; translation of *La Cité grecque*, 1928), p. 26.

II. GREEK TOWN-PLANNING

1. See Ch. I, note 1; and D. S. Robertson, *Greek and Roman Architecture* (2nd edn., Cambridge, 1943, reprinted, 1945), ch. xii. For the most important sites — *Milet, Ergebnisse d. Ausgrabungen seit d. Jahre 1899*, ed. T. Wiegand (Berlin, 1906-36); T. Wiegand and H. Schrader, *Priene* (Berlin, 1904); M. Schede, *Die Ruinen von Priene* (Berlin and Leipzig, 1934).

2. P. 46.

3. W. Judeich, *Topographie von Athen* (2nd edn., Munich, 1931), p. 430.

4. *Hellenistic Architecture*, p. 170.

5. *Klio*, 1928, p. 76.

6. It should be remembered that the buildings on either side, especially houses, were not very high (one or two storeys), so that narrowness was not

so objectionable, and the streets were quite light, especially in the Greek atmosphere.

III. FORTIFICATIONS

1. R. L. Scranton, *Greek Walls* (Harvard U.P. 1941; bibliography, pp. 5 ff. and appendix iii); W. Wrede, *Attische Mauern* (Athens, 1933; magnificent illustrations); von Gerkan, pp. 17 ff, 110 ff.; Fabricius, §§ 8, 9, 24; there are also a number of fine publications of individual sites, *e.g.* Rhys Carpenter, etc., *Defences of Acrocorinth and Lower Town* (*Corinth*, iii. 2, 1936) and two volumes of *Milet* (iii. 2, Berlin, 1922, and ii. 3, Berlin, 1935); Frazer's descriptions of remains are admirable, *e.g.* on Pausanias i. 32. 1, i. 38. 8, iv. 31. 5, viii. 8. 4, x. 32. 8, x. 33. 3.

2. *Sélinonte*, p. 146.

3. See Judeich, p. 120.

4. *Inscr. Graec.* ii. 167; see *A.J.A.*, 1910, p. 298.

5. Scranton, *Greek Walls*, appendix ii; it can be seen at Priene, fig. 6 and Pl. XII (a).

6. R. G. Collingwood in *Antiquity*, vi, 1932, p. 261. See also B. Pace, *Sicilia Antica*, ii (1938), pp. 385 ff., for Sicilian fortifications, not included by Scranton. I have not seen Krischen's *Stadtmauern von Pompeii*, which also deals with Sicilian fortifications.

7. To some extent the strength and grandeur of Greek walls, the massive blocks and careful fitting, are due to a weakness — the lack of good binding materials. Large blocks are used to reduce the number of joints.

8. Packed earth filling was occasionally used (Carpenter, *Acrocorinth*, p. 93, note 2); one important and vulnerable stretch at Corinth has a core of sun-dried brick.

9. *Greek Walls*, ch. ii.

IV. AGORA

1. F. Tritsch, 'Die Agora von Elis und die altgriechische Agora' (*Österr. Jahreshefte*, xxvii, 1932, pp. 64 ff.), is still the best general account of the subject. But the American excavations at Athens are now of vital importance; see reports appearing in *Hesperia* from 1933 onwards, especially vol. vi, 1937, pp. 1 ff., 11th report, by H. A. Thompson, on the buildings on the west side of the agora, and Supplement iv, 1940, on the tholos, etc., also by Thompson; see also note 2 below. For the agora in planned cities see especially *Milet*, i. 6 and 7 (summarized by R. E. Wycherley in *Journal of Royal Inst. of British Architects*, Oct. 1938, pp. 1005 ff.); T. Wiegand, *Priene*, ch. vi, and M. Schede, *Die Ruinen von Priene*, ch. v; for a brief general account R. E. Wycherley in *J.H.S.*, lxii, 1942, pp. 21 ff.; and useful criticisms by R. Martin in *Revue Archéologique*, 1946.

2. Thompson in *Hesperia*, vi, p. 218 ; Martin in *B.C.H.*, 1942–43, p. 281 (this article, on the Stoa Basileios, and another on pp. 348 ff., give useful summaries and criticisms of the American investigations).

3. See Judeich, pp. 62, 285, 296. Dörpfeld (*Alt-Athen*, p. 33) postulates an even older Old Agora, immediately west of the Acropolis, on the saddle between it and the Areopagus, but this is highly doubtful.

4. See Tritsch (on Elis, see n. 1 above, pp. 83 and 92), who again emphasizes Minoan connections. For Dreros, see *B.C.H.*, lxi, 1937, pp. 10 ff.

5. I have accepted in the main the carefully considered conclusions of the excavators themselves in matters of topography and identification of monuments. H. A. Thompson very reasonably claims greater credence for 'the scholar on the spot, who is inevitably more conscious of the stones, the stratification and the levels, and who consequently feels himself bound, often to his own embarrassment, to give more weight to this sort of evidence '.

6. The primitive buildings were unsuitable in plan and dimensions for a meeting-place for the council ; it is suggested that they were offices and the council actually met outside.

7. One would expect the chief fountain of Athens to be in the agora, but one must not beg the question. It has been suggested that the new discovery is really a certain ' fountain among the osiers', near the Council-House (Lycurgus, *Leocrates* 112 ; see Judeich, p. 201). The old claimants are a spring south-east of Athens in the Ilissus valley and a fountain-house discovered and backed by Dörpfeld, west of the Acropolis and near the Pnyx. For the whole problem see Frazer's Pausanias ii, p. 114 and Judeich, pp. 193 ff.

8. Plutarch, *Cimon* 8. 5–7, 13. 8 ; *Theseus* 36. 1–4. The shrine of Theseus was certainly not the so-called ' Theseum ' ; and equally certainly it was not the large rectangular building in the central part of the agora, with which Dörpfeld identifies it (*Alt-Athen*, p. 72). This is the Odeum, a covered theatre of Roman date ; the so-called Stoa of Giants, visible and mysterious long before the recent excavations, belonged to a late reconstruction of its façade.

9. There is abundant literary evidence for these ; see Judeich, pp. 328 ff.

10. *Hesperia*, ix, 1940, pp. 1 ff. It was probably Pausanias' temple of Ares (i. 8. 4).

11. *Hesperia*, vi, p. 53.

12. The arrangement of the north side, now cut off by the Athens-Peiraeus railway, must remain uncertain. Here the Poikile probably stood. We also have references to a ' Stoa of the Herms' (Aeschines iii. 183), which was probably also in the northern part, if indeed it had a separate identity at all, which has been disputed (see fig. 11).

13. Cf. report of paper by C. H. Morgan in *A.J.A.*, xliii, 1939, p. 301. Reports of excavations at Corinth in *A.J.A.* go back to the beginning of the

century. See also vol. i. of *Corinth* (*Introduction, Topography and Architecture*) (Cambridge, Mass., 1932) and vol. i, Part ii (*Architecture*) (1941).

14. H. von Gaertringen, etc., *Thera*, iii, pp. 55 ff. and 112 ff.

15. Including the record office in the Metroön. Full publication and accessibility of records was a democratic institution. Hence the overwhelming number of Attic inscriptions.

16. Social life in fifth-century Athens was mainly informal. Special organized clubs, societies and guilds became more common in Hellenistic times, though the *hetaireia* or social and political club, generally oligarchic, meeting in private houses, played an important part in the fifth century.

17. *Mantinée et l'Arcadie orientale*, p. 186.

18. In Demosthenes (?) xlix. 22 ; cf. Judeich, p. 452.

19. By von Gerkan (p. 94), refuting J. C. Wymer's *Marktplatzanlagen der Griechen und Römer*, Dresdener Diss., 1916.

20. Von Gerkan (who regards this as the normal type — p. 97 — though it would perhaps be more correct to call it a *common* type) and other German writers constantly use the term ' Hufeisen ' ; it is obviously not altogether appropriate (the stoas are more reminiscent of goal-posts, Association type), but it is convenient and may be retained.

21. For the precise relation of the agora and its stoas to the street plan — a very important factor — see von Gerkan, pp. 95 ff.

22. For a brief account of the buildings of Delos see W. Laidlaw, *History of Delos* (Oxford, 1933), ch. vii. See also our Ch. VII, note 18.

23. This important building has at last been carefully and elaborately published by E. Lapalus in *Délos*, xix (Paris, 1939).

24. One might mention here another island agora, at Thasos, the Hellenistic form of which is known and can be seen in our fig. 2. A series of long stoas gave it the form of a slightly irregular parallelogram, almost fully enclosed.

25. Tentative and occasional use of it probably goes back even to archaic times. Weickert (*Typen*, p. 175 ; see also p. 172) lists several allegedly archaic examples, noting as characteristic of these early peristyles a certain irregularity and lack of uniformity between the different sides. That even the regular peristyle is pre-Hellenistic is shown by some houses of Olynthus (p. 188 below) and the building in the Athenian agora mentioned immediately below (see *Hesperia*, vi, 1937, p. 354, and viii, p. 213 ; filling, and overlying remains, indicate a fairly early date for this building). The ' Roman Market-Place ' at Athens, east of the agora (see fig. 1 and fig. 11) is a good example of the peristyle agora-building ; it was built in the time of Augustus and was a market for oil and wine. The second great peristyle court, with exedras, immediately to the north, was built in the time of Hadrian, and the rooms on its east side housed a library.

26. Somewhat fanciful reconstructions of the ' agoras ' of Ephesus used

to be made. See rather *Forschungen in Ephesos*, iii, pp. 89 ff. ; and for a brief account J. Keil, *Führer durch Ephesos* (Wien, 1930), pp. 70 ff.

27. The agora of Megalopolis has been described as Ionian (by G. C. Richards in Supplement to *J.H.S.*, *Excavations at Megalopolis*, 1892, p. 102, and by the present writer in vol. v of the Loeb edn. of Pausanias, p. 64). But though the buildings were placed regularly along the sides of a rectangle, and two long stoas occupied each the greater part of one side, the units had not the close coordination of the Ionian scheme ; open passages ran freely between the buildings and we do not find combinations of stoas.

28. Slight remains have also been found of a late Hellenistic stoa in the eastern part of the north side of the agora, extending to within a short distance of the Attalus stoa. *Hesperia*, v, pp. 4–6, vi, p. 357, viii, p. 213.

29. For the Pergamene stoas see pp. 115 ff. For the Hellenistic form of the Metroön see fig. 36 ; and for the Pergamene library see fig. 7. Record offices like the Metroön are the nearest Hellenic approach to public or official libraries, though literary men, philosophical schools and others accumulated collections. The Metroön housed a very mixed collection of documents, available for consultation ; we hear of copies of decrees, records of law-suits, official correspondence and wills ; the librarian was a public slave. In Hellenistic and Roman times regular official libraries were instituted for study and research. At Pergamon, the library occupied the north side of the precinct of Athena, and contained a large square room, dominated by a statue of Athena at the back, and three narrow rooms for housing the books. This was probably the prevailing Hellenistic type for a large library (see C. Callmer, in *Opuscula Archaeologica*, iii, Lund, 1944), until more splendid and better equipped types were developed in Roman times.

V. SHRINES AND OFFICIAL BUILDINGS

1. See D. S. Robertson, *Greek and Roman Architecture* (2nd edn., Cambridge, 1943, reprinted 1945), ch. iv–x. C. Weickert, *Typen der archaischen Architektur in Griechenland und Kleinasien* (Augsburg, 1929), deals mainly with the evolution of the temple in its various forms. For accounts of important national shrines see, *e.g.*, E. N. Gardiner, *Olympia, its History and Remains* (1925), and F. Poulsen, *Delphi* (translated by G. C. Richards, 1920) ; and the magnificently illustrated work of W. Hege and G. Rodenwaldt, *Olympia* (also their *Acropolis of Athens*). Von Gerkan (pp. 104 ff.) speaks of the place of shrines in regularly planned cities.

2. Contrary to later practice, some early temples have a place for sacrifice and even burnt offerings *inside* the temple. Some temples also were built on the site of or around a pre-existing altar.

3. This is very noticeable at Delphi, where a road like a reversed S leads up from the gate to the temple.

4. 'The Periclean Entrance Court to the Acropolis' (*Hesperia*, v, 1936,

pp. 443 ff.) ; continued in 'The Setting of the Periclean Parthenon' (*Hesperia*, Supplement iii, 1940) and *Hesperia*, xv, pp. 1 ff. and pp. 73 ff.

5. Examples of most of the types will be seen in the plans of Olympia (fig. 27), the Argive Heraeum (fig. 28), etc. Weickert classifies them carefully. R. L. Scranton shows (*A.J.A.*, 1946, pp. 39 ff.) that there were many subtle variations of proportions and interior arrangement, as also of the integration of the inner structures in the surrounding colonnade.

6. *Typen*, p. 167.

7. The most notable example was the temple of Apollo Didymaios, near Miletus.

8. Recent study of this form has mainly centred about the Stoa of Zeus (Royal Stoa ?) at Athens ; see H. A. Thompson in *Hesperia*, vi, pp. 6 ff., especially pp. 53 ff. R. Martin has an interesting study of the winged form in *B.C.H.*, 1942–43, pp. 274 ff. And see article ' Stoa ' by Hobein in Pauly-Wissowa, II. Reihe, Halbb. 7, pp. 1 ff. ; Weickert, *Typen*, pp. 68, 121, 170, 179.

9. Considerable traces of these ship-sheds have been found around the harbours of Peiraeus ; see Judeich, p. 438 ; the ships rested on long stone bases sloping down to the water ; between and parallel to these bases were rows of columns which supported the roof. For another interesting dockyard building, known only from inscriptions, Philo's arsenal (fourth century), see Robertson, p. 182 ; it was a very long (400 ft.) narrow hall, of which the roof was supported by two rows of pillars.

10. *Ath. Mitt.* lv, 1930, pp. 53 ff.

11. G. Leroux (*Origines de l'édifice hypostyle*, Paris, 1913, p. 185) thinks that the stoa is a type of megaron (see p. 180), of which a lateral wall has been replaced by a colonnade ; as in the megaron and its successor the temple, there can be one or two rows of interior supports. This theory is ingenious but I doubt whether there is much truth in it. The stoa is very different in conception from the megaron, particularly in point of openness and accessibility. (I quote Leroux here and elsewhere only to disagree ; but in fact the book is one of the most useful and stimulating on various Greek building-types.)

12. This had the advantage that when, as often happened, the roof and ceiling were pointed and the inner columns carried up to a greater height than the outer, through their slenderness the Ionic shafts did not have to be made disproportionately massive. In single-aisled stoas the roof generally had a single slope.

13. Examples of most of the varieties mentioned here will be seen in the plans of Olympia and the Argive Heraeum (fig. 27 and fig. 28). There was a long and representative series of stoas at Delos, of which a conspectus is given by R. Vallois in *Architecture hellénique et hellénistique à Délos* (i. *Les Monuments*), pp. 160 ff.

14. *Hesperia*, vi, p. 55.

15. See Anderson and Spiers, *Architecture of Ancient Greece* (1927), p. 178.

16. *Corinth*, i (see Ch. IV, note 13), pp. 212 ff. ; some shops of the S. Stoa were taverns, with wells for wine-cooling (*Hesperia*, 1947, p. 239).

17. Council-houses, etc., have been carefully studied by W. A. McDonald in *The Political Meeting-Places of the Greeks* (Baltimore, 1943) ; see also Robertson, ch. xi. I have not yet seen F. Krischen's *Antike Rathäuser*.

18. With K. Kourouniotes, *Hesperia*, i, 1932, pp. 90 ff.

19. See McDonald, *Meeting-Places*, p. 80 ; and H. A. Thompson and R. L. Scranton in *Hesperia*, xii, pp. 269 ff. ; long stoas on top of the Pnyx hill were erected in association with this rebuilding, separated from the Assembly-Place by level terraces (see fig. 11).

20. On the other hand, we read in Plutarch (*Lycurgus* 6) that Lycurgus the law-giver thought that the meeting-place of the Spartans should be in a secluded spot and should have no elaborate adornment, since men were distracted by statues, paintings, the proskenia of theatres (see p. 172) and the elaborate roofs of council-houses. All this is somewhat anachronistic in reference to Lycurgus' time since such meeting-places did not exist so early.

21. I do not propose to enter into the difficult questions of roofing in these buildings ; the evidence is usually scanty and obscure. Probably in the Thersilion and some other large halls there was a clerestory over the central part to give additional lighting.

22. Though McDonald suggests (p. 262) that there was *one* central row of columns, and that the rows of seats were placed at right angles to the main axis. The mode of seating in such buildings is very uncertain.

23. Perhaps containing the statue of Zeus God of Oaths (Pausanias v. 24. 9), by which the athletes swore to play the game. Weickert (*Typen*, p. 66) and others suggest that the square building was an auditorium, but McDonald (p. 231) thinks the walls too light.

24. Thompson suggests (*Hesperia*, vi, p. 150) that it was wooden and rectilinear (possibly polygonal). The fragments of curved marble benches which have been found are late.

25. D. M. Robinson boldly restores certain remains at Olynthus as a council-house with semicircular seating, and a rectangular courtyard in front with a colonnade on either side, thus making it a simpler prototype of the Milesian scheme (see McDonald, p. 233 and *Olynthus* xii, p. 297). But the remains are scanty and the restoration very conjectural.

26. McDonald (p. 254) remarks that the size of council-houses varies greatly and is by no means in proportion to the size of the city ; contrast the Sicyonian with the smallish Athenian. About 26 m. × 20 m. is a favourite size for cities of moderate population.

27. *Édifice hypostyle*, p. 258.

28. See McDonald, ch. vii F, for these secondary uses.

29. *E.g.* by Frazer in *Journal of Philology*, xiv, 1885, pp. 145 ff.

30. Judeich (pp. 63 and 296) speaks of earlier prytaneia on the Acropolis (cf. L. B. Holland in *A.J.A.*, xliii, 1939, pp. 289 ff.) and also in the old agora, but such migrations of the sacred hearth are not likely. For the Tholos see *Hesperia*, Supplement iv.

31. For the Prytaneia of Miletus and Magnesia see fig. 16 and fig. 19. There was a building of similar type in the Argive Heraeum (VII in fig. 28) which Weickert (*Typen*, p. 172) calls a ' Bänketthaus ' ; it is a slightly irregular peristyle of possibly archaic date.

VI. GYMNASIUM, STADIUM AND THEATRE

1. See E. N. Gardiner, *Greek Athletic Sports and Festivals* (London, 1910), ch. xxii, and *Athletics in the Ancient World* (Oxford, 1930), ch. vi ; J. Oehler in Pauly-Wissowa vii, Halbb. 14, cols. 2004 ff. (1912) (see also Oehler's *Das humanistische Gymnasium im Klass. Altertum*, 1909) ; G. Fougères on ' gymnasium ' in Daremberg and Saglio, *Dictionnaire des antiquités grecques et romaines* ; for the Athenian gymnasia see Judeich, pp. 412, 415, 422. For the gymnasium as park and its influence on Roman gardens, see P. Grimal, *Les Jardins romains* (Paris, 1943).

2. Attempts have been made to differentiate ' gymnasium ' and ' palaestra ' more precisely ; *e.g.* it has been said that the palaestra was for boys and the gymnasium for young men, or that the gymnasia were public institutions, the palaestrae private ; but there is only a very limited amount of truth in this.

3. For these examples see Pausanias ii. 10. 1, vi. 23 ; i. 17. 2, viii. 31. 8.

4. See note 1.

5. Rogers' translation. See also Plato's *Lysis* and *Euthydemus* for pleasant scenes in palaestra and gymnasium at Athens.

6. *Édifice hypostyle*, p. 247.

7. There were special bathing establishments even in the fifth century, no doubt of a simple type, such as one recently discovered in the Kerameikos at Athens, with an arrangement for heating water which seems to have developed from a potter's kiln. Hot baths were not unknown. These bathing establishments, as contrasted with the austere gymnasia, were condemned by Aristophanes as the resort of the effeminate ; see especially *Clouds* 837, 991, 1045.

8. Top centre in fig. 17 ; *Milet*, i. 9 deals with the gymnasia, palaestrae and baths of Miletus.

9. This room has benches round the walls, and numerous pupils have scratched their names to mark their places.

10. See E. N. Gardiner, *Greek Athletic Sports and Festivals*, ch. xii, and

Athletics in the Ancient World, ch. ix ; Pauly-Wissowa, II. Reihe, Halbb. 6, cols. 1967 ff. (Fiechter) ; A. Marquand, *Handbook of Greek Architecture* (1909) (useful for other building types too), p. 329.

11. *A.J.A.*, xli, 1937, p. 549.

12. See reports in *Jahrbuch*, 1938, p. 561, and 1941, pp. 1 ff. (I have not been able to get hold of the latter); and *J.H.S.*, 1939, p. 195, and 1938, p. 223.

13. The starting-line was originally a mere line marked on the ground ; its usual classical form was a row of stone slabs sunk in the ground, divided into sections by holes in which posts were set ; between the holes are pairs of parallel grooves to mark the place for the runners' feet.

14. Much work has been done on the theatre in recent years, but in spite of repeated careful investigation of remains the results are discouragingly inconclusive. For a summary see M. Bieber, *History of the Greek and Roman Theater* (Princeton, 1939) (magnificently illustrated ; good bibliography, p. 433). Particularly important are H. Bulle, ' Untersuchungen an griechischen Theatern ' (*Abh. Bayrischen Akad.* xxxiii, 1928) ; a series of studies of theatres by E. Fiechter, *Antike Theaterbauten*, especially Nos. 5 and 7, *Das Dionysos-Theater in Athen* (Stuttgart, 1935-36) ; A. W. Pickard-Cambridge, *The Theatre of Dionysus in Athens* (Oxford, 1946) ; C. Anti, *Teatri greci arcaici* (1947) (this deals with the relation of the theatre to other assembly-places ; I did not receive it in time to make use of it.) W. Dörpfeld and E. Reisch laid the foundations for the study with *Das griech. Theater* (Athens, 1896), and Dörpfeld's views still have to be reckoned with. A. E. Haigh, *The Attic Theatre* (3rd edn. by A. W. Pickard-Cambridge, Oxford, 1907), is still useful for general information about the theatre. See also R. C. Flickinger, *The Greek Theatre and its Drama* (4th edn. 1936). Von Gerkan, p. 107, and Fabricius, § 19, deal with the place of the theatre in the plan.

15. ' Untersuchungen ' (see note 14), pp. 1, 2 and 9.

16. New Pleuron (late third century) had a curiously sited theatre, adjoining the wall and actually incorporating a tower in the stage building.

17. *Greek and Roman Theater* (see note 14), p. 139. ' Classical ' is here used in a restricted sense, meaning fifth and fourth century.

18. But the type was not rigidly fixed and local convenience was the determining factor. Rectilinear or flattish forms, which were perhaps more common in the early phases, were used occasionally even later, the former at Tegea, for example (*B.C.H.*, l, 1926, p. 168 ; here rectilinear seating ultimately gave way to circular in the second century B.C.), the latter at Thoricus (see fig. 44).

19. *E.g.* at Athens, Argos and Syracuse. Wooden benches were no doubt often used in the earlier phases.

20. For criticisms of Fiechter see Broneer in *A.J.A.*, 1938, p. 597 (see also 1935, p. 417), Schleif in *Jahrbuch, Archäol. Anzeiger*, 1937, col. 26, and von Gerkan in *Gnomon*, xiv (1938). Final agreement is hardly likely to be attained

21. Fiechter has a theory that a skenotheke was built at Athens too, probably towards the end of the sixth century. It was a long narrow building just south of the orchestra (it was later replaced by the stoa mentioned below). It formed the backing of the wooden skene and was used for storing timber and properties. Most investigators, however, deny the existence of this skenotheke.

22. This stoa is generally described as a sort of foyer or shelter for the audience in case of sudden rain ; but it was not very large or convenient for the purpose. Its connection with the theatre was by a stairway up into the skene ; it faced south over the precinct of Dionysus, where a new temple was built in the latter part of the fifth century, and it may be thought of as primarily an additional embellishment of the precinct. However, such stoas at the rear of the stage building became common in later theatres.

23. Bulle believes that the stone skene had a low wooden platform above steps between the paraskenia, and that this may even have been so in the wooden skene. This is possible but highly conjectural ; in any case it hardly segregated orchestra and stage.

24. Miss Bieber points out (*Greek and Roman Theater*, p. 219) that architecturally the proskenion is a particular form of a type of structure found in other buildings too (*e.g.* houses at Pompeii and elsewhere) — a flat-roofed portico attached to a higher building. She finds parallels in the East and Egypt. But these need not be prototypes. One need hardly see more in the proskenion than yet another adaptation of the versatile Greek stoa.

VII. HOUSES

1. The recent discoveries at Olynthus are of the greatest importance for the study of the Greek house ; see D. M. Robinson, etc., *Excavations at Olynthus* (Baltimore, 1929-46), especially vol. viii, *The Hellenic House*, by D. M. Robinson and J. W. Graham ; more material has now been published in vol. xii ; vol. x gives masses of interesting evidence for the content and equipment of the Greek house. Professor Robinson has also written the article on Houses in Pauly-Wissowa, Supplement VII, 1938, cols. 223 ff., supplementing E. Fiechter in vol. vii (1912), cols. 2523 ff. B. C. Rider, *The Greek House* (1916), is still useful. For a brief general account see Robertson, ch. xvii.

2. We read of particularly fine and well-furnished houses in the *country*, *e.g.* Thucydides ii. 65. 2 ; Isocrates, *Areopagiticus* 52.

3. Some variety and occasionally adornment would be given to the streets by public fountains, the entrance porches of public buildings, and more commonly by shops ; sometimes the part of a house adjoining the street formed a self-contained shop, not communicating with the house behind.

4. Demosthenes xlix. 22 ; Pausanias ii. 8. 1 ; Thucydides iii. 72. 3.

5. Von Gerkan (p. 91) notes that each block is allowed its full area, and provision is made in the original layout of the site for streets of more than

usual width where they are required ; the framework of the plan is not simply two sets of lines at right angles, but something which requires nicer calculation, two sets of strips, which, though not necessarily all of the same width, form rectangles all of the same size. Where a slice has been taken off the normal house-block this usually means a later widening of the street.

6. For other examples see von Gerkan, p. 92.

7. The type of roof natural to this form of structure was gabled.

8. *Hesperia*, ii, pp. 542 ff.

9. Though it is suggested by Robinson (in Pauly-Wissowa, see n. 1) that the ' courtyard ' is actually a larger room.

10. We are mainly concerned here with the ordinary houses of ordinary citizens. The houses of kings while they survived, and tyrants where they arose, may have been comparatively elaborate. But there was nothing which can be called palatial in normal Hellenic domestic architecture. Interesting specimens of archaic and classical rulers' dwellings have been found at Larisa in Aeolis and Vouni in Cyprus (see Robinson, in Pauly-Wissowa, cols. 251 and 254). Both were built round courtyards and incorporated megara. The Vouni example shows oriental influence (and possible Minoan traditions too), and transcends the normal limits of the Greek house in magnificence.

11. Vitruvius (vi. 7) first describes a courtyard with colonnades and rooms, like an ordinary Greek house ; this is the gynaikonitis (women's quarters). But there is also a more magnificent court with finer rooms around it — the andronitis (men's quarters). Thus it is not so much that a certain part of the house is segregated for the women, as that there is a splendid annexe for the men. There are also minor annexes for guests. The Vitruvian ' Greek House ' represents a degree of elaboration and luxury which very few Hellenic or even Hellenistic houses can have attained. A. Rumpf (*Jahrbuch*, l, 1935, pp. 1 ff.) finds an example of the type in the House of the Masks at Delos, which has been interpreted as a block of four houses, but is really one, Rumpf thinks, containing two courts (the larger would be the andronitis) and two sets of guest rooms ; the layout of the whole complex is very irregular.

12. The term gynaikonitis probably has no special and precise architectural significance. Sometimes no doubt the gynaikonitis may have been a separate court. But in ordinary houses it was probably a single room or several rooms ; sometimes it was on the upper floor ; we also read of its being in an elevated part of the house called the ' tower ', an obscure feature of which the remains tell us nothing.

13. The meaning of this word in classical authors is somewhat ambiguous, but Xenophon, *Memorabilia* iii. 8. 9, seems to justify the use of it. It is not necessary to go into detail about ancient terms for different parts of the house ; usage in ancient authors is often free and confusing ; see *Olynthus*, xii, Glossary.

14. *E.g.* Xenophon, *Memorabilia* iii. 8. 9 ; see *Olynthus*, viii, p. 144. One

could wish that such principles were not ignored so completely by modern builders.

15. Most walls were left in the bare brick ; but a varying number of the more important rooms had their walls stuccoed and painted, sometimes in monochrome, sometimes with one or two zones at the base of the wall in different colours. The zones are sometimes marked off by incisions, and occasionally there are vertical incisions too. Red was the predominant colour.

16. The position of the stairs and other indications lead the excavators to believe that the upper floor usually extended only over the main (northern) part of the house, and not over the east and west wings (though in the Villa of Good Fortune, one of the larger houses standing apart, the position of the staircase shows that the upper storey covered the wings too). There would be a gallery over the pastas, on to which the upper rooms would open. This arrangement accentuated the tendency of the house to turn southwards.

17. L. B. Holland, *Hesperia*, xiii, 1944, pp. 91 ff.

18. Inscriptions also provide evidence for this arrangement, and for the sharing of the ground floor too ; see Vallois, *Architecture hellénique et hellénistique à Délos*, p. 216.

19. See Vallois, *op. cit.* p. 213.

20. Von Gerkan discusses and refutes this view, p. 72.

VIII. FOUNTAINS

1. See especially B. Dunkley, 'Greek Fountain-Buildings before 300 B.C.' (*Annual of British School at Athens*, xxxvi, 1935–36); useful earlier studies are found in *Milet*, i. 5, *Das Nymphaeum*, pp. 73 ff., and by A. C. Orlandos in *Ephemeris Archaiologike*, 1916, pp. 94 ff. For a brief account of water supply generally see von Gerkan, pp. 88 ff., and Fabricius, § 21 ; for Athens see Judeich, pp. 189 ff. *Olynthus*, xii, ch. v, contains much useful material.

2. Glauke is shown in fig. 49. The fountain-house was hewn almost entirely out of a cubical mass of rock. The fourth of the long cisterns had a considerable extension by which the water entered ; the original source is no longer known. Water was drawn from the basins in front. The arrangement of the pillared façade is doubtful.

3. See *Ath. Mitt.*, 1922, pp. 81 ff., pl. VI.

SUPPLEMENTARY NOTES

I. GROWTH OF THE GREEK CITY

1. Two major works on Greek architecture in general have appeared —
W. B. Dinsmoor, *Architecture of Ancient Greece*, 3rd edition, London and
New York, 1950 (full and detailed bibliographies) ; A. W. Lawrence, *Greek
Architecture* (in Pelican History of Art Series), 1957.

R. Martin, *L'Urbanisme dans la Grèce Antique*, Paris, 1956, is of the greatest
importance from the present point of view ; it begins with interesting sections
on laws, regulations and theories.

The *Town Planning Review* of Liverpool has produced a series of articles
on ancient cities, including prehistoric Crete and the Aegean (by R. W.
Hutchinson, XXI, 3, 1950, and XXIII, 4, 1954) ; Hellenic and Hellenistic
Cities (by R. E. Wycherley, XXII, 2, and XXII, 3, 1951) ; and Italy (by
J. Ward Perkins, XXVI, 3, 1955).

In *Urbanism and Town-Planning*, Copenhagen, 1958, a volume of the
proceedings of the Second International Congress of Classical Studies, A.
Kriesis contributes on ' Ancient Greek Town Building '.

On Athens see Ida T. Hill, *The Ancient City of Athens*, London, 1953 ;
and J. Travlos, *Poleodomike Exelixis ton Athenon*, Athens, 1960 (architectural
development of Athens from prehistoric to modern times, with excellent plans
of the city in each period).

Note also Martiensen (Chap. V, n. 1 below), and Bradford (Chap. II, n. 1) ;
the latter makes excellent use of air photography, a method used all too little
in Greece, with notable results on several city sites and also on the lower
slopes of Mt. Hymettus, where he reveals something of the pattern of the
rural landscape which formed a background to the city of Athens.

II. GREEK TOWN-PLANNING

1. Besides the general works given in Chap. I, note 1, above, see especially
F. Castagnoli, *Ippodamo di Mileto e l'Urbanistica a Pianta Ortogonale*, Rome,
1956 ; this pursues the subject in the West and Italy. Axel Böethius, in
The Golden House of Nero, University of Michigan Press, 1960, though
concerned with Roman architecture, looks back to Greek (e.g., pp. 33 ff.,
and p. 187) and discusses the vexed question of the relation of Hellenic and
Italian towns. ' The Greek ideas,' he says (p. 46) ' inspired the Italic town
planners and military architects, but local traditions of symmetry and axiality
and the system of intersecting main streets apparent in early Pompeii make us
expect a special local stamp. . . . If we analyze the earliest regular towns in
Greece and Italy, we must in any case admit that Castagnoli is right in
emphasizing how obvious and dominating the Greek pattern was.'

In *A.J.A.*, lv, 1951, pp. 231 ff. the present writer has added a little on Olynthus (suggesting that the open space at the south end of the North Hill was the agora) and on Selinus. The statement originally made on p. 15 above on planning in the West was too negative. T. J. Dunbabin, in *The Western Greeks*, Ch. x, had already shown that there were fine city-builders in the West, notably at Acragas (Agrigentum), with its series of splendidly sited temples (cf. Castagnoli, p. 22). But evidence of rectangular grids in the earlier periods, and still more of systematic planning comparable with the Milesian type, is elusive and questionable in date.

At Poseidonia or Paestum in southern Italy (see J. Bradford, *Ancient Landscapes*, London, 1957, pp. 218 ff.) the air photographs, confirmed at points by investigation on the ground, reveal an extensive rectangular pattern, with *cardo* and *decumanus* crossing near the central forum, which may be the successor of the agora ; ' on the face of it the buried streets revealed from the air are Roman but may have earlier antecedents '. The great temples, however, lying near the *cardo* and the forum, have a slightly different orientation.

On Peiraeus, *Inscr. Graecae*, i², 887–896 (cf. *A.J.A.*, xxxvi, 1932, pp. 254 ff.) should have been cited. These fifth-century boundary-stones are probably associated with Hippodamus' work and show the care with which sites were marked out.

I. D. Kondis writes of Diodorus' puzzling account of Thurii (p. 21 above) in *Archaiologike Ephemeris* for 1958, and on Aristotle's account of Hippodamus in *Ephemeris* 1955.

On Rhodes see I. D. Kondis, *Contribution to the Study of the Street-Plan of Rhodes*, Rhodes, 1954 (continued in the Greek Archaeological Society's *Praktika* for 1956 and 1959), and J. Bradford in *Antiquaries Journal*, xxxvi, 1956, pp. 57 ff. and *Ancient Landscapes*, pp. 277 ff. The air photos supplement piecemeal observation on the ground and bring out clearly a great rectangular grid, preserved by country lanes and field boundaries, and, more erratically in the narrower limits of the mediaeval and modern town near the harbour, by certain stretches of fortifications and by some streets. The stadium, towards the west, conforms to this plan, running north and south. Two east-to-west streets south of the mediaeval citadel running down towards the harbour indicate the site of the mediaeval market-place, which ' may well have inherited the position of the Agora ' (Pl. I).

On Halicarnassus (and neighbouring sites) see G. E. Bean and J. M. Cook in *Annual of the British School at Athens*, l, 1955, pp. 85 ff. In *A.B.S.A.*, lii, 1957, pp. 138 ff. Cook attributes great city-building activity to Mausolus and the Hecatomnid dynasty of Halicarnassus, affecting perhaps even Heraclea (fig. 9 above) and Priene ; cf. Martin, *L'Urbanisme dans la Grèce*, p. 149. (In *A.B.S.A.*, liii–liv, 1958–59, p. 15, fig. 3, Professor Cook gives an interesting reconstruction of archaic Smyrna by R. V. Nicholls, already with a rudimentary rectangular plan ; cf. *Archaeological Reports for 1959–60*, Hellenic Society and British School at Athens, pp. 40 and 42.)

For a useful summary of the buildings of Pergamon see E. V. Hansen, *The Attalids of Pergamon*, Cornell U.P., 1947 ; and for recent work see the same *Report*, p. 32.

SUPPLEMENTARY NOTES

The recently excavated Sicilian town of Morgantina has a number of interesting features, including an agora with an imposing theatrical arrangement of steps (R. Stillwell and E. Sjöqvist in *A.J.A.*, lxi, 1957, pp. 151 ff., lxii, pp. 155 ff., and lxiii, pp. 167 ff.).

III. FORTIFICATIONS

1. See now Martin, *L'Urbanisme dans la Grece Antique*, pp. 189 ff.

In his book on Athens (see Ch. I, n. 1 above) J. Travlos devotes special attention to the walls and gates, and their location in various periods (pp. 40 ff., where he establishes the approximate line of the archaic wall ; pp. 47 ff., where he accurately determines the line of the Themistoclean wall).

In *Annual of the British School at Athens*, liii–liv, 1958–59, R. V. Nicholls reconstructs from the remains a series of impressive walls of the early archaic period at Old Smyrna, adding a valuable general account of the development of early Greek fortifications. His Wall 3, of the late seventh century (fig. 8 above), was ' fantastically thick ' (the greater use of towers later made possible the use of a thinner curtain) ; behind a face of massive stones were small stones carefully packed in clay. The form of the upper part is not certain, but it was undoubtedly of unbaked brick, probably with the square battlements which became customary in Greece (later a continuous wall with square windows was also used). The platform behind the main wall was laid on the remains of Wall 2, which had a core of brick even in its lower part, as had Wall 3 too in places. Commenting on the comparative meanness of Wall 4 (fourth century), Nicholls says, ' A really efficient and up-to-date defence system was not by any means a luxury in which every city could afford to indulge ' ; the wall of Olynthus was not better than Smyrna 4.

4. *I.G.*, ii, 167, ii², 463, on the construction of the walls of Athens, has been reinterpreted by L. B. Holland, *A.J.A.*, liv, 1950, pp. 337 ff., and F. Winter, *Phoenix*, xiii, 1959, pp. 161 ff.

5. J. Ellis Jones, who with C. W. J. Eliot and L. H. Sackett publishes an interesting example of the remoter line of fortification (p. 44 above), the ' Dema ' wall between Mt. Parnes and Mt. Aegaleos (*Annual of British School at Athens*, lii, 1957, pp. 152 ff.), maintains that the ' indented trace ' continued in use longer than Scranton allows.

6. In contrast with Collingwood, A. W. Lawrence, *J.H.S.*, lxvi, 1946, pp. 99–107, thinks that the advanced system of the fort at Syracuse is not due to Dionysius but is as late as the time of Archimedes, late third century B.C.

8. In a very fine wall at Gela in Sicily much of the upper section of crude brick is still in place, and has now been given a plastic covering (see *J.H.S.*, Archaeological Reports, 1956, p. 53 ; *Illustrated London News*, 26.1.57, p. 155).

IV. AGORA

1. R. Martin, *Recherches sur l'Agora Grecque*, Paris, 1951, deals exhaustively with the architectural form of the agora and with its political, commercial and religious life.

On the agora of Athens see continued annual reports in *Hesperia*, and for a concise summary, *The Athenian Agora, Guide to the Excavations*, Athens, 1954 ; the present writer has made a new collection of the ancient evidence in *The Athenian Agora*, Vol. III, *Literary and Epigraphical Testimonia*, Princeton, 1957, and given an account of the market district in *Greece and Rome*, 2nd Series, iii, 1, 1956, pp. 2–23.

3. See now R. Martin, *L'Agora Grecque*, pp. 256 ff. ; J. Travlos, *op. cit.* Ch. I, n. 1, p. 28. I am now inclined to believe that there was indeed a primitive agora immediately west of the Acropolis.

7. See further *Hesperia*, xxii, 1953, pp. 29 ff., xxv, 1956, pp. 50 ff. ; cf. *The Athenian Agora*, Vol. III, p. 140, and Ch. VIII, n. 1, below.

13. A further volume of the American publication of Corinth, I, Part iii, *The Lower Agora*, by R. L. Scranton, Princeton, 1951, clarifies our picture of the Corinthian agora and gives improved plans ; see also Ch. V, n. 8, below. The present writer has given a brief account in *Journal of the R.I.B.A.*, Nov. 1953, pp. 1–4.

17. On the ' agora of the gods ' see R. Martin, *L'Agora Grecque*, pp. 169 ff.

24. R. Martin has begun a full publication of this important agora in *Thasos, l'Agora*, Fasc. I, Paris, 1959.

28. Cf. *Hesperia*, xx, 1951, pp. 53 ff. The new ' South Stoa II ' replaced the stoa mentioned in p. 60 above ; a short ' East stoa ' joined its eastern end to that of the long ' Middle Stoa ' ; thus an almost distinct square was formed south of the main agora ; this has hitherto been labelled ' Commercial Agora ' (see especially *Hesperia*, xxii, 1953, pp. 35 ff.), but Professor Homer Thompson tells me he now has better reason to believe it was used by the law-courts, in close conjunction with the ancient court adjoining it on the south-west.

V. SHRINES AND OFFICIAL BUILDINGS

1. R. D. Martiensen, *The Idea of Space in Greek Architecture, with special reference to the Doric temple and its setting*, Johannesburg, 1956, gives an original treatment, from an architect's point of view, of the planning of Greek shrines ; cf. R. Scranton, *Group Design in Greek Architecture*, Art Bulletin (College Art Association of America), xxxi, 4, 1949, pp. 247 ff. ; Scranton gives a careful analysis of the varied relations of temple, stoa and other elements. See also Kondis on Olympia (fig. 26 above).

2. On altars, see C. G. Yavis, *Greek Altars, Origins and Typology*, St. Louis, 1949.

8. R. Martin discusses the form of the stoa and its part in the planning of public places, shrines, etc., in *L'Agora Grecque*, pp. 449 ff.

The South Stoa at Corinth (see p. 62 and fig. 14) has been fully published by O. Broneer in *Corinth*, Vol. I, Part iv, Princeton, 1954. He dates its construction in the latter part of the fourth century B.C. The shops had inner rooms ; many of them were wine-shops, as is shown by their contents, and by the presence of wells, fed by a conduit from the fountain Peirene and presumably used for wine-cooling. Above the shops was a row of rooms facing south on to a corridor, possibly serving as a kind of hotel.

The Stoa of Attalus at Athens has been completely rebuilt to serve as a museum (see H. A. Thompson in *Hesperia*, xxvi, 1957, pp. 103 ff., and *The Stoa of Attalus at Athens*, Princeton, 1959). The terrace in front (a common accompaniment of these long stoas), which served as a promenade and view-point for processions in the agora, has also been reconstructed.

The stoa at Thasos (p. 114) is now restored by Martin (see Ch. IV, n. 24 above) with a facade of columns instead of walls in its wings.

10. The reconstruction of the South Stoa in the Shrine of Hera at Samos (fig. 29) gives a good idea of the primitive forerunner of the classical stoa. The plan is clear ; the supports were wooden posts, the upper structure is a probable restoration. G. Gruben gives a good account of the evolution of the stoa (*Ath. Mitt.*, lxxii, 1957, pp. 61-2).

13. On Delos and its interesting early stoas see now H. Gallet de Santerre, *Délos Primitive et Archaique*, Paris, 1958.

31. A house at Eleusis has been reasonably identified by Mr. Travlos as the Prytaneion (see plan in *A.J.A.*, lx, 1956 ; fig. 41 above). Two large rooms on the north side of the court, with accommodation for couches around the walls, were no doubt the dining-rooms ; the long narrow room to the north may have housed the sacred wagons.

VI. GYMNASIUM, STADIUM AND THEATRE

1. J. Delorme gives a full account of the history, architectural form and functions of the gymnasium, with illustrations of most important examples, in *Gymnasion, Étude sur les Monuments Consacrés à l'Éducation en Grèce*, Paris, 1960. Cf. H. Marrou, *History of Education in Antiquity*, transl. G. Lamb, London, 1956, p. 67.

The gymnasium of Delphi has received its final publication in J. Jannoray and H. Ducoux, *Fouilles de Delphes*, II, *Le Gymnase*, Paris, 1953.

Work is now continuing in the neighbourhood of the Academy at Athens. Reports appear annually in the *Ergon* of the Greek Archaeological Society. Little has been found even now of the gymnasium buildings of pre-Roman time, but a considerable stretch of what appears to be the early enclosing wall of the Academy has come to light. The present writer gives an account of the gymnasia of Athens in a forthcoming article in *Greece and Rome*.

The group of buildings north of the archaic temple at Corinth (fig. 14) is tentatively interpreted by Scranton as a simple kind of gymnasium, with a long stoa facing north on to a terrace, and a curious kind of bath-house to the east (*Corinth*, I, iii, 1951, p. 179).

On gardens see Mrs. D. B. Thompson in *Archaeology*, IV, 1, 1951, pp. 41 ff.

11. A *dromos* or race-course is restored on the base of this starting-line in fig. 14. The Panathenaic Way as it passed through the agora of Athens may also have formed a kind of *dromos* (see J. Travlos, *op. cit.* Ch. I, n. 1, p. 70).

12. Work at Olympia has continued to add to knowledge of the peri-

pheral buildings, including the stadium. Besides the series of *Berichte über die Ausgrabungen in Olympia*, E. Kunze gives a useful conspectus of results in the German Archaeological Institute's *Neue Deutsche Ausgrabungen*, Berlin, 1959 ; he notes (p. 267) that the fifth century race-course was further west and extended right into the shrine towards the altar of Zeus, whereas the late fourth century stadium was further east and more detached.

14. T. B. L. Webster, *Greek Theatre Production*, London, 1956, though mainly concerned with details of production, also deals briefly with the building, e.g., pp. 4 ff.

The theatre of Corinth has now been fully published by R. Stillwell, *Corinth*, Vol. II, *The Theater*, Princeton, 1952, and its history is of particular interest.

A new and greatly enlarged edition of M. Bieber, *History of the Greek and Roman Theater,* has appeared (Princeton, 1961).

VII. HOUSES

1. The houses of Olynthus have been discussed, e.g., by A. Boethius, *American Journal of Philology*, lxix, 4, 1948, pp. 396 ff. ; J. W. Graham, *A.J.A.*, lvii, 1953, pp. 107 ff., *Hesperia*, xxii, 1953, pp. 196 ff., xxiii, pp. 320 ff. and xxvii, 1958, pp. 318 ff.; and the present writer in *Journal of the R.I.B.A.*, liv, 3, p. 135 and lvi, 10, p. 439.

More satisfactory material is now available at Athens itself, mainly from the fringe of the agora area (cf. p. 196 and fig. 48). Professor Rodney Young has published ' An Industrial District of Ancient Athens ' in *Hesperia*, xx, 1951, pp. 135–288. The area is south-west of the agora and was largely occupied by marble- and metal-workers. In very general type the fifth and fourth century houses found here are like those of Olynthus, being built round a small court, which tends to be on the south ; and their construction is similar. But they do not have colonnades, or any such marked and characteristic features as the Olynthian *pastas*; they vary in size, and both houses as a whole and individual rooms are irregular in shape. More recently Professor H. A. Thompson has published a group of similarly modest fifth century houses on the narrow streets running down from the north foot of the Areopagus towards the agora (*Hesperia*, xxviii, 1959, pp. 98–103 ; cf. the present writer in *Journal of the Royal Institute of British Architects*, May 1961).

Mr J. Ellis Jones has recently investigated an interesting Attic country house, built round a more spacious courtyard (near the wall mentioned in Ch. III, n. 1 above ; report forthcoming in *Annual of the British School at Athens*).

On the equipment of the Athenian house the inscribed records cf the sale of the confiscated property of Alcibiades and his companions are especially important ; W. K. Pritchett concludes that ' there was little sense of personal luxury in Athens in the last quarter of the fifth century, even among men of wealth ' ; and, ' by modern standards, certainly the Greek house must have been relatively empty ' (*Hesperia*, xxv, 1956, pp. 210, 212.)

SUPPLEMENTARY NOTES

Interesting Hellenistic houses, with evidence of Hippodamian planning, have most recently been coming to light at Pella in Macedonia (for brief preliminary reports see *J.H.S.*, lxxix, 1959, *Archaeological Reports for 1958*, p. 13 ; *B.C.H.*, lxxxii, 1958, p. 761, and lxxxiii, p. 702).

VIII. FOUNTAINS

1. For the fountains of Athens see now fig. 13, fig. 24, and Pl. XVI(a), and Ch. IV supplementary n. 7. The archaic S.E. Fountain had rectangular water basins at either end of a rectangular area. The fifth century S.W. fountain had an L-shaped basin behind a porch of the same shape. The agora *Guide* (see Ch. IV supplementary n. 1 above) has a useful section on water supply.

INDEX

Figures in brackets refer to supplementary notes.

441947